ABOUT
GUMP RECORD

We began with a simple observation. We noticed that we, as architectural learners, repeatedly prove great strength in our abilities to design and communicate our designs to peers. But, this often overshadows and hinders the necessity of observation and experimentation beyond our desks. Without an ability to step outside our own creations through observation and experimentation, our work lacks relevance in the course of human history. To firmly understand where we have been, where we are, and where we are going, we are reaching beyond the boundaries of our studios. We are wielding new instruments. We are seeking new understandings of foreign processes and methodologies. We are learning from those on the frontiers of innovation.

To begin this discourse within our intimate community, we asked a small group of contributors to choose their own topics to investigate through a series of articles. This is not a group of experts; this is a group of architectural learners willing to reach beyond their prescribed curriculums. They each chose a topic that stirred their initial passions and curiosities, distilled it to its essence, and then nurtured it to deeper levels of clarity and relevance.

This publication is the compilation of their investigations and observations. By recording their processes, frustrations, and successes, we hope to inspire others to individually explore and learn from our contributors.

CONTENTS

SOUND
EVAN DANCHENKA

Evan is a current third year architecture student and Levine Scholar at UNC Charlotte. He consistently listens to a large variety of 20th century music and has written several self-invested, experimental compositions. Naturally, his music theory background pours over to an architectural education. His spectrum of interest ranges from surreptitious sound phenomenons to programmatic, calculable sound designs. Evan chose to write about sound for Gump Record to begin a discourse with designers on similar abstract wavelengths of thought. His main goal is to inject awareness of sound into an overly visual realm. By learning to listen, one experiences space, relationships, and memory in a whole new way.

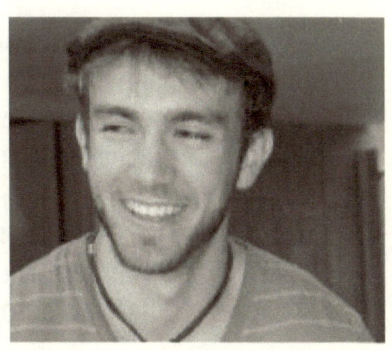

HOW DO I LISTEN?

Every fifteen minutes for the past 157 years, the four bells of Notre Dame de Paris have chimed loud and proud, resonating through the streets. This year, these historic bells are being replaced with eight new ones. Some Parisians believe this will permanently alter the city's aural identity. The replacement is like an attempt to sing while using someone else's vocal chords. Memories attached to the sound of the old bells are now in danger of being lost.

> This debate showcases just how deeply embedded sound is in creating a sense of place.

I am convinced that sound plays a critical role in defining that sense of place, and I welcome you to join my studies on the idea. Learning how to listen to architecture, just as one has learned to see architecture, is an essential tool for the aspiring designer who considers how a place should come to be.

How do I listen?

Experimental composer John Cage once stood in a fully sound-absorbent room and heard a loud throbbing pulse in his ears: the sound of his own pumping blood flow. Place yourself in a similarly silent environment, and you too might hear your yourself in a similarly silent environment, and you too might hear your own pulse, counting the beats by listening, instead of touching. Aware of these powerful aural abilities, you can practice listening to the built environment in the same way.

First, the listener should begin noticing directions sounds come from, the durations, and the distance they travel. Down a hallway, across a room: how long is the hall?

Close your eyes, because your ears will tell you first.

Next, beautiful, musical tones will start to cut through the white noise. With practice, one develops instinctual recognition of these tones, and can associate a sense of atmosphere with them. Think of phenomenology (the study of consciousness and the objects of direct experience).

Then, the listener tries to compartmentalize the sounds and the experiences attached to them. Categories are made in the mind through the ear.

And suddenly, the urban environment starts to become much more clear, distinct, and wondrous -- ah, the sense of place has revealed itself!

Now, to sort through this confusing premise, let us imagine some simple scenarios:

1. You are walking along a busy market street and the chime of a distant church bell suddenly cuts through the chaos. You immediately recognize it as the St. Thomas Aquinas church bell. Further, you notice it strikes three times - three o'clock. You might think to yourself, "What a beautiful layer of sound added to my experience in this market." Then someone turns to you and asks, "Excuse me, but do you know the time?" Of course, you know! - because you are an experienced listener

(and this stranger obviously is not). It's three o'clock, and you look forward to four o'clock, wondering what the chimes will sound like from a different location.

2. You find yourself in an old arts district of town. On your last visit, you noticed something pleasant and sophisticated about the people, but you couldn't put the observation into words. Now, with your new trained ears, you notice the soft rise and fall of the voices of outdoor diners suddenly sounds more like a babbling brook, serenely trickling over the clinking chinaware: a refined and noble sound--not just a conglomerate of indiscernible words. Visit another arts district and another town, and the brook might turn into raging rapids!

These aural characteristics are innate qualities of what make each place uniquely identifiable.

> As a designer, one can tap into these sound identities and create real architecture around them

—walls that leak out sounds while strategically letting in others; gathering places situated where sounds pleasantly blend in musical harmony (sometimes very literally); and even complex geometries meant to bend and reflect sound in the most unexpected ways. These are the ideas that I shall study and lead us through over time. |

"And like visual proportions, the more complex the combinations are, the more admirable the aural result."

PROPORTIONS OF SOUND AND ARCHITECTURE

"Architecture is frozen music." – Johann Wolfgang von Goethe (1749 -1842).

To the visual scholar, such as an architecture student, this quote might not make sense. You may have heard it before and feel that it is true, but are not sure why. My initial reaction was to imagine a row of giant columns shaped like bass drums, frozen in place. Others might have dreamed of dancing transoms or singing roofs. Doesn't this piano-and-violin building (below) epitomize "frozen music?" We know it doesn't, of course. It is a gimmick. Our instincts tell us that "architecture is frozen music" means more.

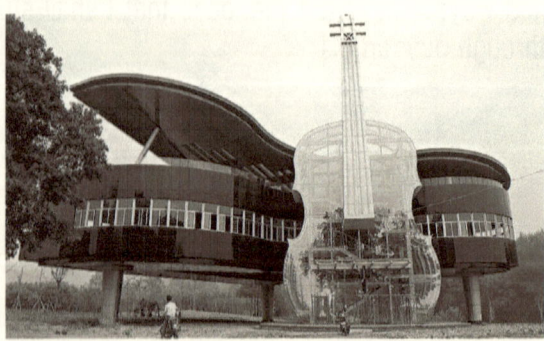

Both composers and architects have referred to the idea before and after Goethe: Stravinsky, Varese, Xenakis, Alberti,

Palladio, Corbusier, and Zumthor, to name a few. The common thread through all of their explanations is one simple rule that I will focus on in this brief article: Proportion.

Visual
As architecture enthusiasts, we know that proportion is a relationship between smaller parts of a greater, logical whole. When our eyes recognize order in a building, we might feel a sense of pleasure derived from familiarity—much like when you see a friend's face. We like what we recognize. So, we call repeating halves "rhythmic," the law of thirds "balanced," the nine-square "centralized," and Phi, 1.618 "golden." The more complex the order is, the more we admire it, right up to the moment when cognition finally fails us, and we can no longer recognize a proportional logic.

Give any architecture student a Palladio building, for example, and he or she will immediately recognize the quarter-divisions, the right angles, and the square bounding lines. But, give them an Eisenman building and see the baffled look on their face as they begin to sort through the complexity in search of order. If they finally discover it, their sense of achievement is much sweeter.

Aural
For the music enthusiasts, we also know that proportion is a relationship between smaller parts to a greater whole. We recognize proportion with our ears.

> The same proportions that are pleasing to our eyes are, in fact, the exact same in music.

There is no grand mystery between the two. As Alberti said, "The same numbers, by means of which the agreement of sounds affects our ears with delight, are the very same which please our eyes and our mind."

Both sensory phenomena are measurable. If a 4-inch line doubles in length to 8 inches, so does the frequency of Middle C 261.626 Hz to Tenor C 523.251. The doubled frequency makes an octave, and all the notes C# through B proportionally make up what is in between. These proportions combine to make chords and all other musical phenomena. And like visual proportions, the more complex the combinations are, the more admirable the aural result.

Below are descriptions of accompanying music composed based on each visual example. To listen to each example, visit **gumprecord.org/evan-danchenka.**

Tartan Grid

This grid is an overlap of thirds and fourths in both horizontal and vertical directions. The music sample represents the horizontal reading in rhythm, first playing the halves (bold black lines), then quarter divisions (bold black/dashed/bold black/dashed), then thirds (bold black/thin black/red/thin black). The verticals represent pitch, climbing by a fifth and forth (bold black lines) and landing on octaves (top and bottom black lines). More pro-portions fill in at the end (dashed lines).

Façade Reading

The drawing of this building can be read as a musical score, though there is really no correct way to do so. If we were to walk across this building from left to right, the same direction as you would read music, the follow-ing sound sample would result: The small columns are represented in a rhythm that duplicates every three beats, and the roofs proportionality stack to create chords heard over the rhythm. Notice how the entrance changes the rhythm of the sound and the height of the roofs changes the pitch of the notes. |

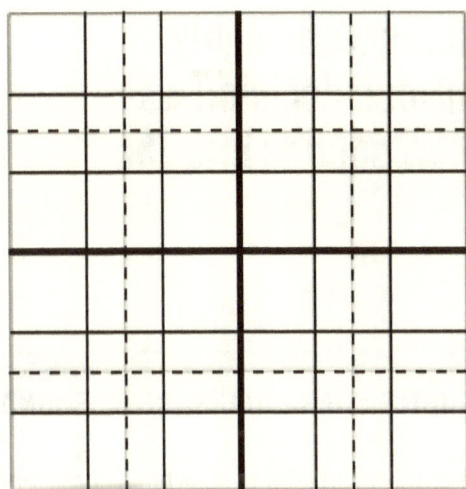

Tartan Grid

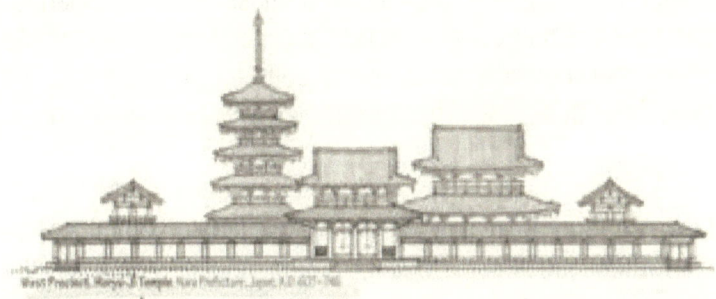

West Precinct, Horyu-Ji Temple, Nara Prefecture, Japan, A.D. 607–746

Façade Reading

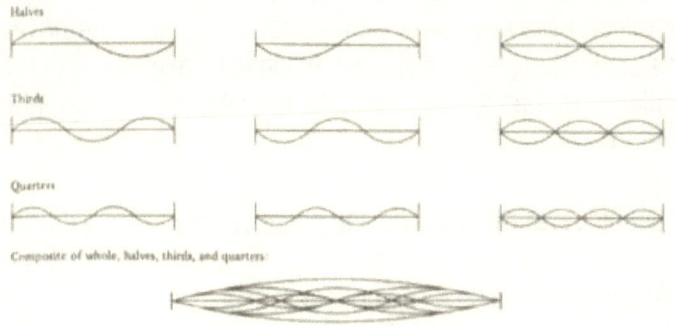

Halves

Thirds

Quarters

Composite of whole, halves, thirds, and quarters:

Musical proportions shown graphically

"This tells me that the sounds were highly considered and a conscientious decision was made to introduce these new sounds into the city fabric."

THE SUBTLE CHARACTERISTICS OF SOUND

This article gives real-world examples of just how important the characteristics of sound are in our everyday built environments. Often subtle and overlooked, these "sound scenarios" can have great effect on a person's experience of a place. As a designer, consider what sound does in the place you are building or designing. These examples will show what I mean:

The Vehicle
Luxury car companies employ a special kind of sound technician whose job is to choose the sounds that go into a vehicle. These technicians work solely on the beeps, buzzes, pitches, and tones that a driver will hear every time they climb in, start up the engine, turn on the radio, flick the turn signal, and adjust the air conditioning. These subtle characteristics often go unnoticed by a new owner for months. But once the novelty wears off, the owner will start to obsess over the beautiful subtleties of the car, and hopefully not nitpick over any shortcomings.

For instance, someone is driving home on a sweltering day and the air condition is humming on high. At a red light, the owner flicks on the turn signal and notices that the "tick-tock's" coming from the dash are working in harmony with the humming air conditioner. The tones are actually quite pleasant and soothing, exactly what the day required. This is nothing like that junker the owner previously drove. You know, the one that squealed when the windows rolled down or honked like a baboon when the horn sounded.

These sound characteristics make a qualitative difference between the designs that are successful, and those that are not.

Home Improvement Stores
I usually enjoy the sounds of a home improvement store, large or small. I hear music in the beeping excitement of scanners, forklifts, and trucks, in the dragging of chain links, and in the clanging of lumber and steel.

The sounds give character to the place, suggesting all of the materials available to me at once,

while my ears work through the chaos to decipher where things are. Lately, however, I've heard complaints from people about a big-box home improvement store. They sense something annoying or distracting about the place, but no one has been able to pinpoint why. Curious, I ventured in to take a listen.

On either end of every isle were two security cameras and their accompanying screens. Each time a customer walked by them a high-pitched, "ding-ding" quickly sounded off. I isolated the sound of one of them, and noticed that the two pitches were a pleasant major third apart--C and E, or maybe G and B. The real problem, however, was that each security camera's "ding-ding" was slightly different from the next. In effect, when all of the security cameras were going off at once, they blended together in a most dissonant clash, echoing off of the concrete floors, and bouncing through the hardware merchandise. Imagine an orchestra tuning before a performance where all the instruments are slightly out of tune. When used properly in music, dissonance can be quite beautiful, full of tension and richness. But, in a Home Depot, it is a nuisance and a distraction.

Public Transportation

I have observed sounds of public transportation across the country, and there is one example in our backyard, the Charlotte Lynx line. Although the bells and whistles of the light rail are not actual bells and whistles, they do work well together. This tells me that the sounds were highly considered and a conscientious decision was made to introduce these new sounds into the city fabric.

This is what you hear.

The "ding-dong" of the opening and closing door is the major third A# and D. The repetitive cross arm "ring-ring-ring" is an octave D higher at some stations, while a high G at others. D and G are a nice 5th apart. Lastly, the train bell is a high F. Together, all four pitches of the Lynx light rail can be abstractly thought of as an A# major chord, or a Gmin7 chord, as well as other chord configurations. The point is, no matter the chance arrangement, all of the sounds work harmoniously together, and add a very pleasant sound texture to Charlotte. The tones even sound soft and subtle, suggesting the youth of the light rail and the niceties it affords passengers. Play those notes on a piano and you will hear them. Better yet, go for a ride on the light rail, or go for a stroll down the tracks.

But, if you can't do either one of those, listen to the accompanying sound montage using recordings of the light rail. I play other chords over top of the light rail sounds in order to show just how much opportunity for play there is in the sounds that our light rail gives us. To listen to this montage, visit **gumprecord.org/evan-danchenka**. |

MARTIN BRESSANI

INTERVIEW WITH MARTIN

Martin Bressani is an architect, an architectural historian, Associate Professor, Associate Director, and Graduate Program Director at McGill University's School of Architecture. I interviewed Martin following his lecture at UNC Charlotte on February 20, 2013. Below you will see my questions and has paraphrased answers to these questions.

What do you consider to be atmosphere? Is it literally the moisture in the air or a collection of activated senses?

Atmosphere is not in terms of the ambient qualities in a technical sense. It's more of the affective qualities of a space. In the lecture, Bressani uses the example of a charged atmosphere where you feel it as if you are entering something solid. People usually generate this atmospheric quality. He believes that architecture has a role in setting up these affective landscapes in the room. He states that it is a decorative take, on some level (while acknowledging the term's superficial connotation); but clarifies that as architects, we are answerable to these qualities. This includes aspects like the temperature of a floor because that alone can create certain senses of space. But he is more interested in affective presences in a space, the "haunted," that one can engage with. These are not resolved in the form of the room. They are, instead, the totality of "formal givens" that generate a unified environment in which you enter and have an affective presence. He believes that it is important to become aware of these aspects. That means that there are perhaps certain ways of representing space. Specifically, he speaks of integrating renderings into the process of design in a way that allows these qualities to emerge and become engaging.

So, understanding this is less of a scientific process and more of an intuitive process?

Bressani states that it engages your sensibilities; so, it is truly artistic in that sense. There are not any objective criteria. But he believes it is not subjective; people have completely different experiences within the same space. But, he believes there is a certain objectively given affect that we can all agree upon. Though, there may be things that attract some of us, distract some of us, or might just be boring for others. "It's like reading a novel: we can all agree upon the plot of the novel, or what the novel is trying to do." But someone might find the novel uninteresting while it changes another's life. Essentially, it exists as an object, as a story. It has a certain objectivity. But, there is an interpretive dimension. His argument is that the atmospheric qualities of a building are a fictional dimension; it's that thing that transports your moods. Atmosphere has the power to change moods, and therefore mentally brings you somewhere else. You may not embody that mood yourself, but you can recognize it within the space. The architect decides that whatever activity takes place in that room should also take place in that particular atmosphere. Bressani believes there are appropriate atmospheres for every space. The character of buildings, the feel of buildings, should be appropriate to the program and demographics of the building. Bressani calls it the "occasion" or "social situation" that the building is about. He recognizes that atmospheres can change when, for example, a warehouse evolves into an artist's loft. In this situation, the post-industrial abandoned feeling pleases the artists. They feel liberated there; they can do certain things there. It doesn't just fiscally accommodate a struggling artist, but the space provides an appropriate atmosphere for the new occupant. Now, contemporary museums are deliberately built as warehouse spaces because artists have conceived their work in those spaces and they want their work to be shown in those spaces.

Do you push your students to define atmospheres?

Bressani tells them, "let's begin a project by envisioning feelings, raw feelings." So, they take a photograph of a site that analytically portrays a tone. Then, they envision a building within this photograph. So, the photograph interprets the site. Out of this capturing process, he states that the building "appears to your eyes. It's very literal." Students then create an architectural tone to intensify and condense. From there, they start making architectural decisions that are more definite. Then, the students coordinate the connections and details. Essentially, all of these steps follow the authority of an ambiance. "Does it serve the tonality I am trying to achieve?" Bressani states that in the history of architecture, many of the beginning sketches by architects are actual drawings of their buildings, not abstract diagrams. Often, it is a vision of the building. That vision, for him, entails a certain architectural sensation that to which we should listen. He questions if we can organize affective space: are there spaces for melancholy, are there tragic spaces, and are there festive spaces? He admits that this topic is very unclear and fuzzy.

"In the method of collaging the site context imagery, where might sound, or even organized degrees of sound, such as music, play a part in the process? Is sound ever an investigation or product of this iterative architectural study?"
-- Question by Evan Danchenka

"Yes, it is." But Bressani states that sound is difficult to measure, model, and see. Since architecture is such a visual art, students work visually with drawings or models. We could technically model sound as we model parti diagrams; but the architect's talent is in abstraction through plans, sections, elevations, etc. Though orthographic drawings, we can begin to accurately engage the building spatially. We could walk through it and feel it—as if site reading space. It is like a good musician who is able to listen by reading the score. He goes further in mentioning that the acoustics of a space, based on materials, are delicate. For him, the atmosphere is a total system of resonances that include sound, touch, light, time, etc.

He also said that he is interested in media artists who project onto buildings. Bressani dislikes when media installations are too much like a movie screening where the architecture merely provides a backdrop. He reiterated, from his lecture, his belief that we should become media architects. "How does a building communicate? How do buildings relay information?" He admits this requires a complex answer; but the way a building engages people physically and emotionally is part of its communicative power. We communicate, in a detailed and technical way, how we allow our buildings to be seen and experienced. Bressani thinks that appearances are critical because they are interpretations of institutions; they can create ideal scenarios.

How do you think the fiction or playfulness of a design is conveyed in what is actually constructed?

Bressani believes architecture is excess. When an architect is called in, it's usually because the client is ready to spend money on something. "You could say that's pretty crass." He clarified by saying it's when we care about a place that we are willing to be excessive about it. Therefore, a market is a very affective site. Whereas, if you are doing a "hum-drum" building, he states, all that is considered is the economy of that building. There's no question that an architect can be useful in this situation. But, he thinks that an architect's true role is to redistribute excess. He says to his students that these imaginative projects are what get them jobs when they go to interview with their portfolios. He states that architects, invariably, are more interested in these imaginative projects than by-the-book architecture. Usually, good architects work where there is extra money available and focus on iconic places. "[Future employers] call the architect and say, 'we want something special.'" In that sense, Bressani does not see these imaginative and fictional projects as unrealistic. Those projects served as the spark of imagination within future clients. He addresses that build projects have always favored demographics with more resources. He says he is okay with this because people that care about certain things are willing to spend money on them.

Additionally, he believes architecture is something that transports us. Architecture should be something that lifts us. Bressani thinks that a building can create an alternative world; it has a world-creating capacity. But, he does not necessarily believe that a building must be expensive to achieve this. In fact, he tells his students that the more minimal they are with achieving atmosphere, the more powerful that atmosphere becomes. It takes confidence and thoughtful creativity to be able to reduce enough so that an essence still exists. |

WATER, PUBLIC SPACE, AND ARCHITECTURE
KEIHLY MOORE

Keihly grew up along the shores of Lake Superior in northern Minnesota then went to Iowa State for her undergraduate degree in Architecture and Environmental Studies. She followed her passion for energy efficiency and affordable housing to Passive House Institute US (PHIUS). She jumped to UNC Charlotte where its Urban Design program opened doors to a new world of design. She has relished thinking about cities as well as the various systems and intricate human patterns that overlap and intertwine.

Her topic is broadly spurred by climate change. But she realized that before climate change, one has to get to the core of the issue--visibility of natural systems and changes in our urban environments. Water management is hidden in cities--piped and pumped away. It is seen as either a burden when it floods or as ornamentation. Her project aims to bring storm water to the surface, so the public may get a better appreciation for this resource. "Instead of spending millions of dollars on infrastructure we never see, why not bring it to the surface where we will actually benefit from it during the dry periods?"

She believes we need to start thinking about future changes in the climate, which means more extremes, more droughts and more frequent severe storms. "In order to adapt we need to layer our infrastructure within our dense city systems. These measures can only be better for the city and quality of life."

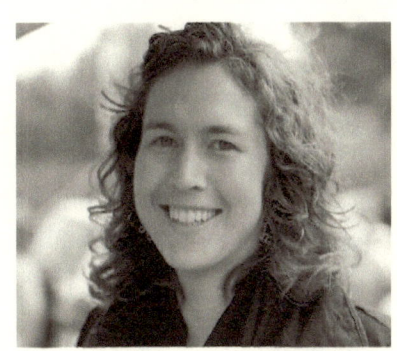

SPARK

The spark of an idea, that is. Usually they come by surprise. Recently, I was lucky enough to get a spark from Russell Thomsen's IDEA Office lecture. It is exciting when a visual stimulant merges with your mind's constant wheel-spinning to form a new idea. It's like a sneak peak into the future. The idea is veiled in a different form, then all of a sudden, it makes sense in a new way you see applicable to your own project. For example, the metal wall forming the facade on the street --the void creating the garden--in the 2008 V-House triggered my imagination. I especially liked the clever conclusion of the wall, the forming of a bench, as it hovers just above the ground. I could see how this type of articulation could be translated into my own project, morphing to fit my own design intentions.

Imagine a new kind of downspout. Imagine an extended channel that carries the water off the roof, and instead of going straight to the ground, it reaches closer to the sidewalk's edge and bends to form a seat at its base on the dry side.

This fusion of water, public space, and architecture is my focus.

My aim is to make water a feature, to make its process and inherent changes visible.

How can architecture and public space facilitate this movement? How can we design for the destruction water normally brings? How can water shape space and become more integrated and appreciated in our daily life? How can these inquires simultaneously contribute to healthier water sources and natural environments? A series of additional questions arises in these early design days:

- How can design convince someone to do the "right thing" by simply making it easy to actually do the "right thing?"

- How can unfortunate events or situations be turned into benefits or opportunities?

- How can thinking outside the profession bring new ideas into territory we aren't normally a part of? |

"I also think it's a valuable exercise to fit a new water system into the existing urban fabric framework – working off of typical distances like standard building measurements and tree placements."

WEAVING WATER IN A NEW URBAN CONTEXT

CriticalMASS was held rooently. It's the UNC Charlotte School of Architecture's annual symposium inviting eleven southeastern architecture schools to present their thesis work. After presenting, I realized that one key to a good review session, and frankly, good conversation, is imagination. When you're seeing something for the first time, I find it's interesting to absorb the ideas, but then to think of its extended potential. What new form can this seed of an idea take? Is it going in the right direction? Where does it need to jump the tracks into a new, more promising, direction?

Often, as designers, we need to think about the future.

> How do you imagine design under a different political situation, different values, or different norms?

I think, for some, this is hard to wrap one's mind around. And this is where my design project comes in. Enter a world where the cost of water isn't cheap, drought threatens in the summer, and flash flooding occurs more frequently. How can capturing this resource, cleaning it, slowing it, and showing it impact city dwellers so they can feel the presence of something ever changing, registering and measuring the ephemeral qualities that affect our environment?

As a designer, I think of a different future, imagining a Charlotte where grey water is reusable, where there is political will to support public infrastructure, and where people are treated as equals amongst cars on the streets.

One set of solutions I propose encourages the design of a facade to not only craft the path of water, but also to slow its running, store it for later, and meet the ground in a way that benefits the public realm in an interesting, helpful way. Is that so much to ask? As it turns out, yes. There are few facade precedents that I've been able to find that can articulate water in a meaningful, useful way. Of course that is due to cost-benefit, and managing water is much more efficient on the horizontal plane. Very soon, an answer in the form of a facade will be designed.

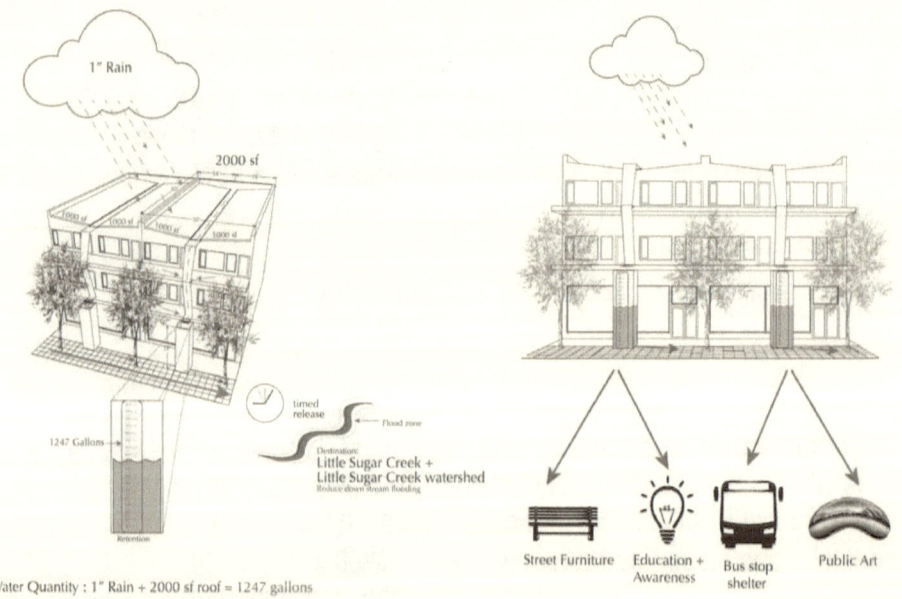

Water Quantity : 1" Rain + 2000 sf roof = 1247 gallons
Sidewalk Cistern : 4' x 4' x 15' = 240 cu. ft | 1793 gallon capacity
Working within design standards to integrate water collection into the urban environment.

These diagrams explain the urban sidewalk cistern, and how it integrates into the facade and street. The sidewalk cistern has the potential to be integrated as seating, a bus stop shelter, public art, and a didactic purpose.

I also think it's a valuable exercise to fit a new water system into the existing urban fabric framework -- working off of typical distances like standard building measurements and tree placements. For example, retail buildings are usually 60 feet deep and street trees are usually spaced 30 feet on center due to canopy growth. How can one element take on multiple roles in the urban environment? (see opposite page, bottom)

Now, to move from the vertical surfaces of an urban street to the horizontal components. Think of a bioswale or rain garden. These ground features already fit into a Best Management Practice (BMP) toolkit. But they don't seem to be very popular in urban environments, partly because they take up valuable space. So why not save space and integrate water's spatial needs with people's spatial needs? Allow a perforated grate panel (derived and randomized from a water pattern) to cover the water and plants that clean the storm water running off the street. It's a walkable rain garden, or a walkable bioswale...a bioswalk? Perhaps.

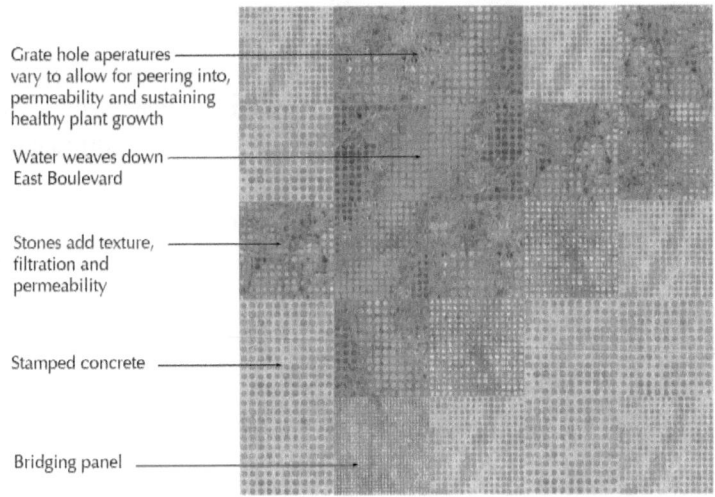

Grate hole aperatures vary to allow for peering into, permeability and sustaining healthy plant growth

Water weaves down East Boulevard

Stones add texture, filtration and permeability

Stamped concrete

Bridging panel

A bioswale or rain garden covered by a custom grate allows people to see into the water system while inhabiting the sidewalk. Water and occupants now layer in a vertical datum.

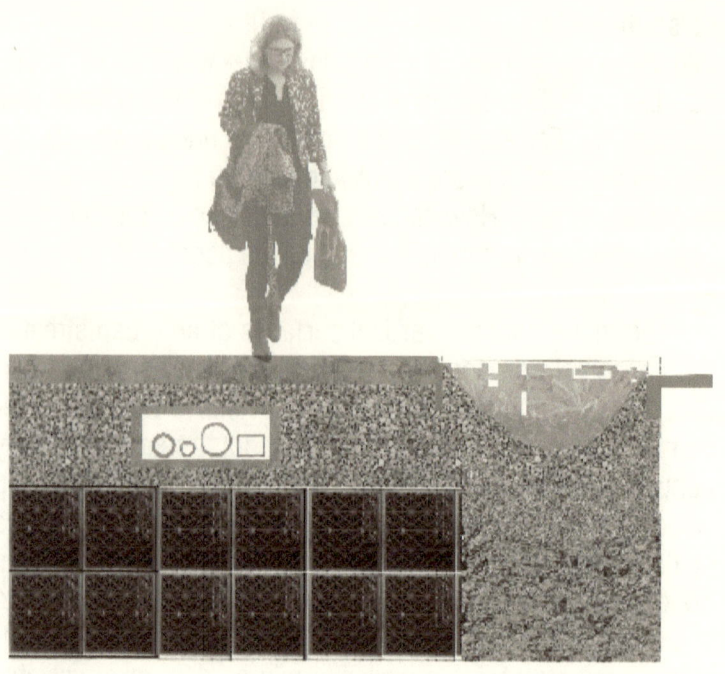

A bioswale or rain garden covered by a custom grate allows people to see into the water system while inhabiting the sidewalk. Water and occupants now layer in a vertical datum.

In the last weeks before my final presentation, I will be working on connecting the vertical facade plane to the ground plane. The key is in the transition and connection joint between the two, tying the public space realm into the private realm, weaving a visible element of water into each. |

"For me, it was an immediate example of how our buildings and infrastructure can withstand or crumble under the force of nature."

REFLECTION: IDEA FROM SEED TO REALIZATION

I think my last article deserves reflection about process over this year. My endeavor started with a look into a rising and flooding sea level in a Philadelphia Delaware River urban design studio project in Fall of 2011.

> The ideas grew into grand visions of how to save towns from flooding, how to buffer storm surges, and how to create sea walls that make place, instead of dividing it.

How could you develop "flood proof" buildings along a street so that a "flood safe street" corridor could be made? Well, of course, the nature of water is so unpredictable; these are hard measures to design for. We also forget that water picks up undesirable substances along the way, and as much as we remember it for its beauty, its waves hold power, destruction and danger.

Then came Hurricane Sandy in late October 2012. It was perfect timing for my research, frankly. Here was a storm that turned our fears into reality. Our infrastructure and system weaknesses were quickly found and exhibited. And, by storm measurements, it didn't even have the strongest winds. For me, it was an immediate example of how our buildings and

and infrastructure can withstand or crumble under the force of nature. Our vulnerabilities were humbling.

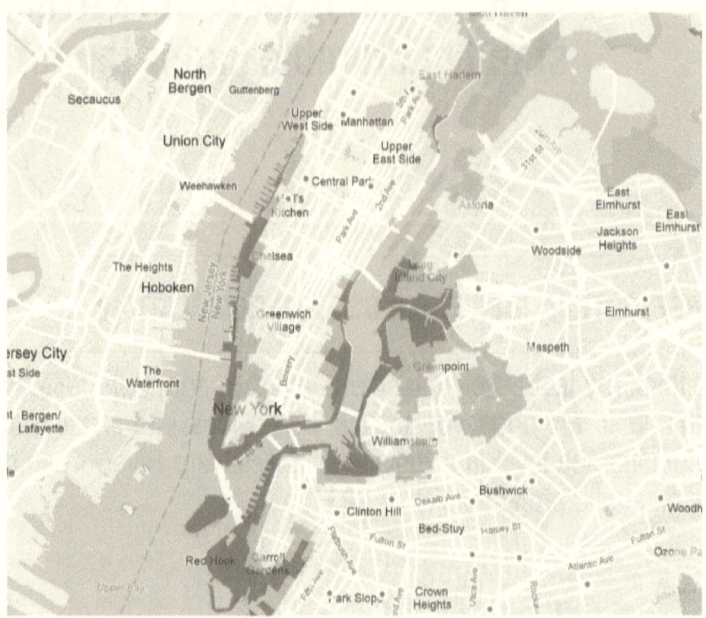

Evacuation map during Hurricane Sandy.

After Sandy, I became much more aware of the broader problems linked to flooding. They go beyond design into policy, disaster management, and safety. Addressing this kind of flooding seemed too huge to approach for a design thesis.

The next pivotal question in thesis, after the topic, is choosing a site. The unpredictability of floods paired with unique geographic locations means that there is no easy answer. I looked into the urban flood walls of Richmond, VA, Wilmington, NC, Norfolk, VA, and New Orleans, LA. Wanting to focus in urban areas, I realized that most of our visible water management happens away from cities. In cities, it is all underground. Much of the existing, above ground flood infrastructure often divides neighborhoods and creates urban blight. Surely there is a way we can design differently.

Venturing away from coastal flooding and tidal influences, I started focusing on inland flooding issues. Charlotte is certainly not immune from these troubles. Urbanization maps show how the area has rapidly grown in the last 40 years. In fact, across the nation, "the rate of increase in impervious surfaces has exceeded the rate of population growth by 500% over the last 40 years."

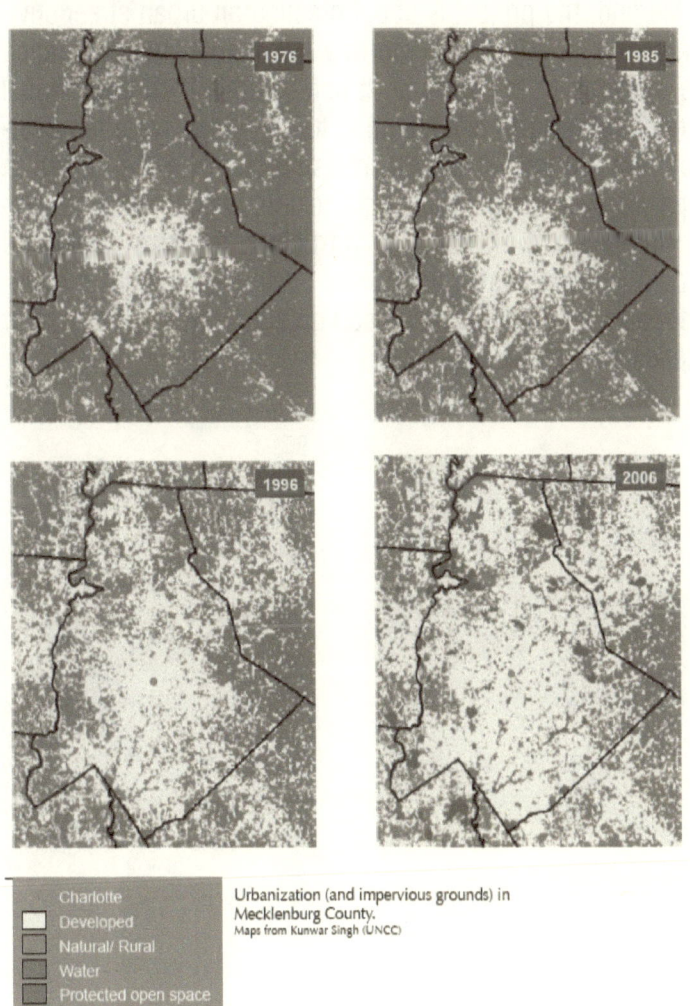

Charlotte
Developed
Natural/ Rural
Water
Protected open space

Urbanization (and impervious grounds) in Mecklenburg County.
Maps from Kunwar Singh (UNCC)

Urbanization patterns in Mecklenburg County. Data from Kunwar Singh, UNCC.

I finally chose Charlotte because of its urban flooding issues and local access to data. I chose the particular area of East Boulevard because of its close proximity (1100 feet) to the Little Sugar Creek (one of the major watersheds in Charlotte), its underdeveloped urban patterns, and the pedestrian populations are already frequenting the sidewalks.

In the end, my project is about creating an urban street environment with a focus on storm water management, bringing the systems to the surface. It holds within it an educational agenda, striving to call attention to the things we often overlook. We are trained to hide infrastructure. We are trained to separate everything. With a little design, the immense amount of money spent on these infrastructural systems could and should actually benefit the public, adding to the built environment as a whole. Integration can go a long way. A balance of poetics and practicality, I say. |

LETTER FOR BIRKENAU

RESPONSE FROM EVAN DANCHENKA

Wednesday's lecture by Russell N. Thomsen of IDEA Office began as any other; an architect presented a collection of projects over his office's career that gave insight into their ideas and processes. But at some point along this role call, something changed. The slides darkened and the release of information about the last project slowed in pace. Russell was careful to ensure that every possible thought behind this project was conveyed with utmost clarity. The project he presented was a radically distinct proposal for the memorial of Auschwitz II–Birkenau.

A project of this nature that so boldly confronts one of the greatest tragedies in human history practically demands discourse!

So, we asked for thoughts on IDEA's proposed project. Evan Danchenka answered the call:

Though having never been to Birkenau, I deeply understand the power of closing it off to the world in the spirit of Tel Olam. This is a very sincere and highly considered statement about people, about memory, and about mourning. What makes Thomsen's idea so compelling is the time scale. For now, mourning is directly observed by the survivors, relatives of victims, and the rest of the very immediate degrees of separation from the atrocities. In hundreds of years from now, mourning will be more for the greater human race who come to Birkenau to experience the magnitude of death and evil in a different kind of way. If Birkenau and other concentration camps remain open, maintained as museums, and Hollywood-ized, then all the significance would vanish, unjustly creating a void in the lessons and translations for our future generations to understand. When the lady described the Colosseum as a grand object and not as a place where atrocities occurred, she did so because of the readily available visitation. "Give me your ticket, in you go, and don't forget the gift shop on your way out."

Tel Olam fills that void in the lessons and translations for future human beings by, in fact, establishing a very real one.

When we are confronted with intangibles in an otherwise extremely accessible world, our generation is already taken aback.

"What, you mean I can't have that?" Or, "What do you mean, I can't see it?" In the future, these confrontations with something intangible will only grow stronger, as the world spins faster and faster, a network of information at our fingertips. Everything is important. Nothing is important. And when future generations cannot access a place like Birkenau, then perhaps they will begin to understand that, when measured against all of the mass mounds of information they will have available, the very disallowance of an experience is that much more real and rightfully disturbing than anything else.

My critique for Thomsen is not so much about the logistics of his formal design, as this will develop as more hands are involved. What I want to say, however, is that Tel Olam must, must, MUST become his entire body and soul to just MAYBE put this brilliant idea into action. Thomsen must focus the entirety of his life on these steps to realization, and nothing else. The passion he exhibited, and even his trepidations, will need to translate into a thick skin he knows he will need. He must cast all other pursuits aside. Tel Olam is Russell Thomsen's purpose.

Though this pursuit may seem bleak, I am more cautiously optimistic than anything. While the subsequent politics and bureaucracy will be brutal from all directions, many great projects realized by the most seemingly unexpected people: Maya Lin, a Chinese-American who built the Vietnam Memorial; John Roebling, a German who built the Brooklyn Bridge, L'Enfant, a Frenchman who designed the plan of Washington, DC. Though these are American examples, they are important precedent models for how Thomsen may be the unlikely candidate for creating Tel Olam. Eisenman, an American, did build the Memorial for the Murdered Jews of Europe (Berlin), and appears to be supporting Thomsen's idea.

In all, it doesn't matter that Thomsen is an architect from Los Angeles. If he were somebody else with a different nationality and a different career focus, criticism would come just the same, only with a different twist.

It takes an exhibition of passion and conviction from the person with the idea.

As for me, I am convinced that Tel Olam is the worthy pursuit. It is the historical, contextual conclusion that will fester a stronger and stronger impact into an overcharged future, refreshingly opposite than any other kind of memorial I know of today. |

RESEARCH THROUGH MAKING
EMILY DALLMEYER

Emily is a Master's student in the M1 track, who studied Sculpture and Spanish at Washington University in St. Louis and earned a BFA in 2007. Since then, she has been making art and working for a variety of non-profits. For the last four-and-a-half years, she has been at Habitat for Humanity of Charlotte, first in construction as an AmeriCorps member and then on staff as the Grant Manager. You might guess from her background that she is interested in social and environmental justice as well as the process of making objects.

For this project, she applied for a grant through the Digital Arts Research Center (Research Through Making) to design and create an installation piece. She is building a wall that folds to demarcate space and is made of component joint and planar pieces. The rectangular planes are shallow reliefs meant to be engaged from 2 - 10' away while the entire installation can be understood from much farther. The exact configuration of the components can change with each installation.

She chose this project as a way to explore space making and composition. She thinks this is a valuable project because it is an opportunity to confront materiality that we do not get to interrogate at the scale of a model. Through this making project, she is addressing design intent and integrity while also fabricating a final object, instead of simply specifying the rules for an ideal object.

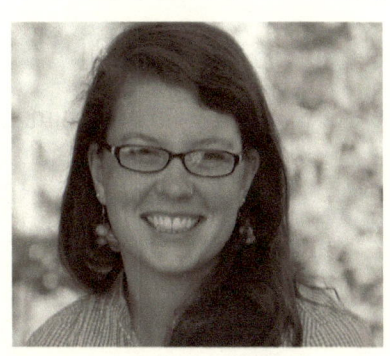

THE BEGINNING

Sometime while at the University of North Carolina, you will write a research paper. Every student is asked to identify a topic, sources, and a thesis; then the research follows. Hopefully, things you read in your sources can be used as building blocks to make an argument or observation. For some this process is engrossing and for others it is painful.

I am also pursuing research, but my process has different steps. The project I first called "Basic versus Fundamental" is based on looking at sources and also based on experimentation through making. Because of the element of experimentation, my project has more in common with the science courses I took in high school than with my research papers.

> Instead of being a paper, the final product will be a constructed wall and a series of articles; of which, this is the first.

It is important to know that the materials for this project (up to $500) are paid for by the Digital Arts Department within the School of Architecture as a part of their larger Research through Making grant program. In fall 2012, a call for proposals went out and I submitted this project. There were a number of other projects funded, and I hope that some of you will submit proposals when the next round is announced.

To put it simply, I intend to use a laser cutter and CNC router (both digitally controlled tools) to make 25 wooden shallow relief compositions that when installed together as a wall affect and create space. Driving this final product are four goals:

- To examine how "basic" compositional exercises can inform the fundamental concept of making space.

- To learn to use the digital fabrication tools and exercise those skillls

- To repeat and explore foundational compositions

- To develop a module that can link together to build a space-making structure.

These goals are really the heart of my research, and their sum will be represented in the final constructed piece. When writing a research paper, you also examine, learn, repeat, explore and develop throughout the process.

Already I have examined building precedents and created a full scale model in wood and cardboard. Before the end of January I will have prototype sheet metal connectors and prototype plywood panels. These two making exercises teach me about the materials, specifically how they behave, how they can be connected, and how the weight of an object affects the connected objects.

In a way it is a design problem, but the building of actual objects makes it research.

Instead of reading a fact, theory or expert argument in a scholarly journal, I have collected data about the physical world. I will use the data that I gather through making prototypes to design and build my final construct. This action parallels the use of facts to hone and then construct support for a thesis. |

"I learned that our professors are right: there is so much to be learned from models."

THE NEXT STEP

My previous goal was to be in the fabrication stage of the physical installation, but my progress was a bit delayed.

One important thing to note is that when I began this process, the compositions of the panels felt like the central element, but as I began to work on the project, I realized that the connections between the panels should inform the compositions on the panels. Currently, I am trying to finalize this linkage piece, while exploring different iterations, in order to determine exactly how the joint informs the surface of the panels.

Early in January, I began collecting quotes on plywood around Charlotte, I bought sheet metal and drew several versions of the linkage for these wooden compositional pieces. I arrived in the fabrication lab, ready to use the plasma cutter (a computer controlled laser suspended over a flatbed that can make 2 dimensional cuts through sheet metal) and upon showing my drawings to Ryan Buyssens, I was heartily encouraged to cut them on the laser cutter in chipboard first and then test them on the metal break (a tool for bending sheet metal) to make sure what I was describing was possible. Long story short, on our tools, it would not be impossible; but it would be difficult, time consuming, and probably not worth it to fabricate my design. There is truth to the axiom "work smarter, not harder."

So I took a step back. I began working at a smaller scale; I reconsidered my overall structure and presented a model at 1/8" = 1" scale. I learned that our professors are right: there is so much to be learned from models. I presented a model, chipboard joint experiments and my reactions to them both at our review in January. When I presented thoughts for my next steps, I asked for feedback and criticism to guide those steps.

My reviewers challenged me to consider some of my basic premises. One suggestion was to make the entire wall out of metal. The more difficult question to address dealt with the nature and purpose of the wooden panel. I have not resolved the relationship between the composition and the shaping of created space. I plan to take a few more cracks at making these stand-ins more meaningful before I abandon them.|

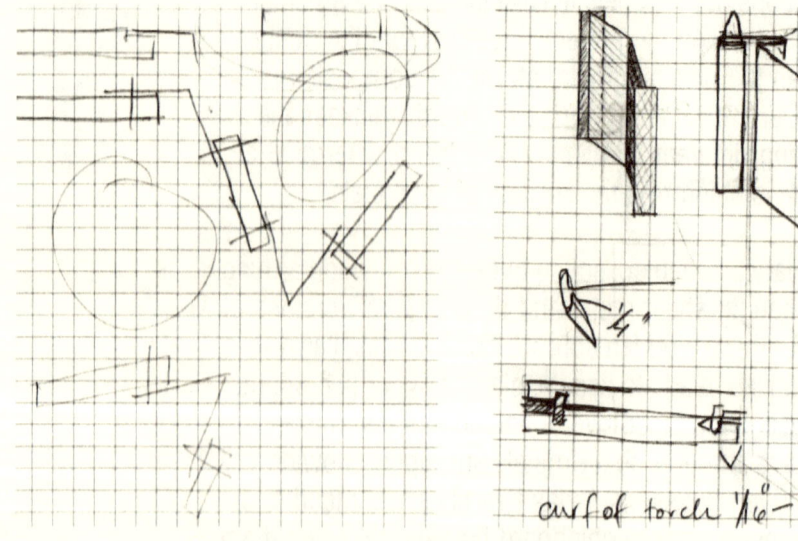

Above, Left | *This is my first sketch of my next stage. It is in plan again, but I have done away with the t-shaped bend in my joint piece.*

Above, Right | *This is a series of sketches for the form of a joint piece. I discovered, when I cut it in chipboard, that it would be nearly impossible for me to create this in our shop with metal.*

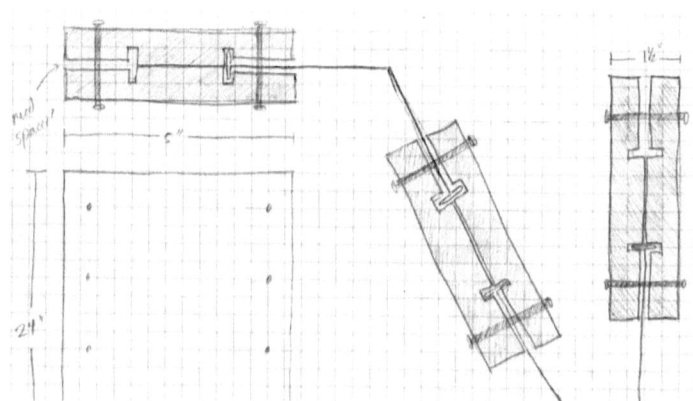

Above | This is a plan drawing that combines the ideas in the previous drawings. I found that if I needed bolts for vertical alignment, I didn't gain anything by bending my metal joint pieces for horizontal alignment.

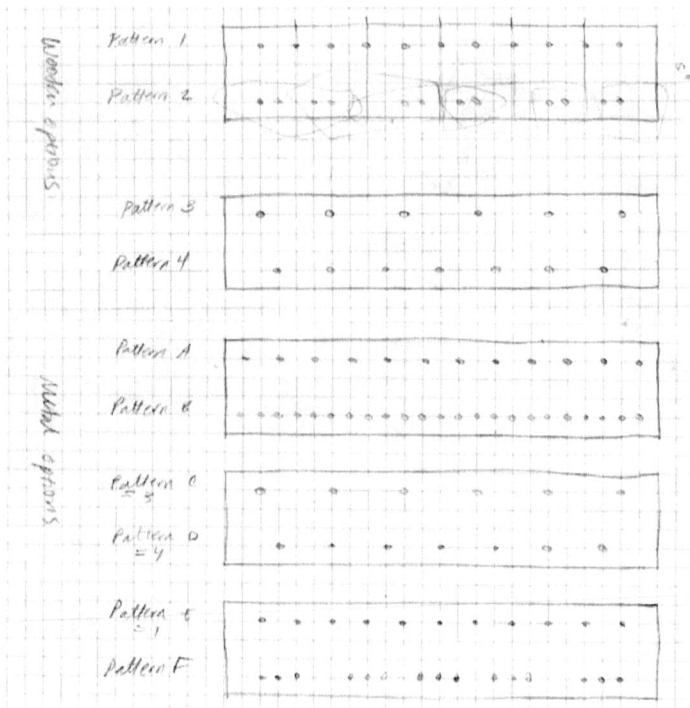

Above | In this pattern study I'm looking at joints that could allow for more variation in the final constructed piece, namely a simple pattern that allows for variation without having extraneous bolt holes.

NEGOTIATING
THE GAP

PROMPT BY KEIHLY MOORE

Today, Friday, February 8, a design charrette was held with design students from Deb Ryan's class and the "neighbors" --folks from the Urban Ministries homeless program involved in an art project at the center. This collaboration is a chance to start a conversation about homelessness in Charlotte and to get creative ideas for how to improve lives of the homeless in the city. A student is paired with a neighbor, each with the task of creating a sort of dream shelter. The student builds a model after talking with their neighbor and, in the meantime, the neighbor does a painting of it. Both will be shown in the front window of the Center City Building in Uptown.

My goal is to start a conversation for those in the class (and others!) to share their impressions and experience of this interaction with their neighbors. What were your thoughts going into this project, how did the conversations you had affect you, and where are you now? How do these conversations change the way you think about the city? How do you think differently about "basic needs" of living? What surprised you?

I'll start. Here are a few phrases that really caught me.

They spread things all over the city. They do not have an anchor. They sleep on the train and even take advantage of free coffee at Harris Teeter. I don't think I want to catch my tears that way; being moved around, moving; no privacy; having few possessions makes things easier, I destroy less.

It had been a while since I had sat down next to someone new, listening to them, winnowing out their personality, their passions, their peculiarities and trying to turn these abstract ideas into architectural form.

How do you translate thoughts into form? How do you encourage them to draw their ideas? How can you encourage creativity in solving their problems?

I also thought more about "basic needs." Have you ever gone without running water? I have for 2 weeks, showering with a bucket, etc. Sometimes we don't realize we need it until we don't have it. My neighbor, in his house, prefers to have a couch. This is all that he needs. Simply nothing else. It is also suspended by the ceiling; he doesn't want to touch the ground, so the entry is through the roof. I have a feeling these ideas are coming from deeper experiences.

I also saw was how quickly everyone started talking to each other. I didn't feel that typical awkwardness at the start of things (tell me if you felt differently).

I also felt that the relationship was cultivated based on the act of listening. Our role, as designers, is to listen and gather, then act. In my interactions, the listening part seemed to be very appreciated and valued.

What are your thoughts and impressions? Is your viewpoint changed? How? |

RESPONSE BY CHRISTINA DERISO

Before class last Wednesday, when we first met with Christa, I was incredibly nervous about this assignment. I have had minimal contact with homeless people and I am often uncomfortable around them when I'm in the city. I was worried I would not be able to help, I was worried I might have a drug addict, I was worried about the awkwardness, I was worried about everything. But, after our discussion/presentation with Christa, and especially the reminder that they are people, I felt better about my meeting.

When I met Miss Vanessa, I was overwhelmed with emotions. It was life changing. She is a wonderful person who has a great, bubbly personality that lit up our conversation. I felt horrible for any of my previous doubts/fears with this assignment, but I also felt hopeful for change. Vanessa has medical disabilities that led to her time being homeless, but she was joyful and excited to talk about her dreams. It was humbling to be put in charge of envisioning her dreams and attempting to make them materialize, even if only in model form. This whole experience reminds me to take time to think about what's truly important in life. As much as things may frustrate me, they are often minuscule and unimportant.

I've had an emotional year, I almost lost my younger brother. Listening to Vanessa, someone who has lost custody of her children, been divorced twice, and was homeless for about two years reminded me of how much everyone struggles; however, her attitude was optimistic in that as long as she continues to work hard she will one day achieve her goals. |

RESPONSE BY CHARLES KANE

"Homelessness is Hell. Being Homeless is like living in Hell."

Those were the last words that my 'neighbor' wanted to share on the questionnaire. She, unlike some of the other partners, recently escaped homelessness. I thought this was an interesting perspective because it made her somewhat hesitant to revisit these experiences. I found my neighbor to be very emotional, engaging, and inspiring, but at some points during our conversation, she was guarded and disinterested.

When we began the design charrette, she immediately suggested a tree house--later deciding she didn't want to have to climb up to a treehouse. She reasoned for the treehouse because of the views that she could get at the tops of trees. However, it seems more likely that she was trying to find security and remove herself from the harsh environment she experienced. In her short explanation of her homelessness, she described how she slept in abandoned houses around Charlotte. She qualified that by saying she would always find a secluded room on the top level of the house. She was searching for security in an otherwise threatening environment.

Once we began to get into more detailed aspects of her ideal shelter, she adopted more of an interested observer role. She enjoyed the ideas we came up with together but did not want to participate too actively. Again, I think her position as an apartment dweller made her unwilling to fully engage in some aspects of the project.

I was very moved by this experience. I appreciated when my neighbor offered a glimpse into her life; despite her guarded nature, she enjoyed having an attentive audience. I look forward to the next meeting with my neighbor and hope she benefitted from our conversation like I did. |

FORM IS FORM
DAKOTA PAHEL-SHORT

Dakota is a third year architecture student in UNC Charlotte's architecture program. Architecture has been a longstanding interest for him, but his main artistic media before college was sculpture and abstract drawing. His studies in architecture have been mostly explorations of form. These studies include how light interacts with different types of surfaces and materials, how form responsibly deals with program, and the interaction between people and form. These explorations have led me to explore many methods of representation of form from digital to physical modeling. His end objective is to be able to put the desired goals of a client into form and to create spaces of play and investigation for those who enjoy the new and unexpected.

His topic of discussion for Gump Record will be the objectives of form that he has concluded as of this point; and he does wish for this to be a discussion. Speak with Dakota if you have an objection or need clarification about any topics he discusses. He chose this topic because he believes we should be more avidly discussing the objective conditions of form so that we can establish more concrete formal rules that allow us to express our own personal objectives in design. He states "Form is a language that should be very intuitively read. We inhabit space all the time. We just have to pay attention to the little details we ignore as a result of repetition. These formal rules allow us to 'write' our desired experiences in form."

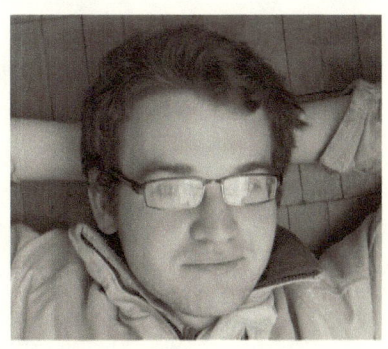

AESTHETICS AND ORDER

We must first ground our footing in visual aesthetics and the creation of order before we talk about the more abstract concepts of creating form and dealing with complex geometries that lie beyond orthogonal hierarchies. To tackle the rules of aesthetics and order, we will simplify them down to several key terms: contrast, layering, alignment, proportion, scale, and grid. These are of course major simplifications, but even the proper application of each of their simple definitions provides a thoroughness and depth to our compositions.

> As designers, however, we should always challenge ourselves to question any absolutes.

That includes any mentioned in this writing. Please, do not take that to mean these absolutes have little value; we simply cannot allow our minds to settle or be inactive. As architects, we must create and then selectively break systems with an eye for aesthetic beauty.

Contrast
Every action has an equal and opposite reaction. This fact of physics is the most basic way of describing contrast. We recognize the power of contrasting elements to divide space and create striking visual compositions. There are dark and light,

heavy and ethereal, black and white, rough and smooth, complex and simple, dynamic and static, private and public, old and new, strong and soft, woman and man, dirty and sacred, grain and cross-grain, additive and subtractive, and a continuing list of conditions that contrast each other. These conditions hold strength within their respective pairings but work even more powerfully when grouped together. The simple, rough, heavy, static, cross-grain, subtractive masonry is a wonderful contrast for the complex, smooth, ethereal, dynamic, dominant grain, additive metal and glass materials. Yes, it's a mouthful; but paired together they are extremely effective at dividing spatial conditions and creating tension. Contrast creates, then reinforces threshold through combining like pairs of contrasting elements. The tension of these clashing elements creates wonderful moments of transition because they suggest a discontinuity of space on the edge they meet.

The main issue of contrast is balance. These conditions must maintain an even 'weight' in the composition in order for the contrast to be apparent. The monolithic nature of the Egyptian

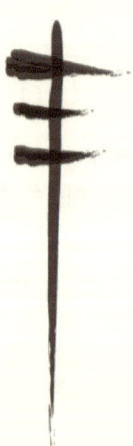

Establishing a dominant grain (direction of alignment) and then balancing it with a cross-grain is another form of contrast. This system is great for creating halls that the program branches from.

pyramids cannot be contrasted by the complexity of a pocket watch. These elements need to be sized so that they can be compared. This does not mean that they need to take up the same amount of space or even be similar elements. The viewer only needs to be convinced that the weaker of the elements is strong enough to influence the stronger of the elements for the contrast to work properly.

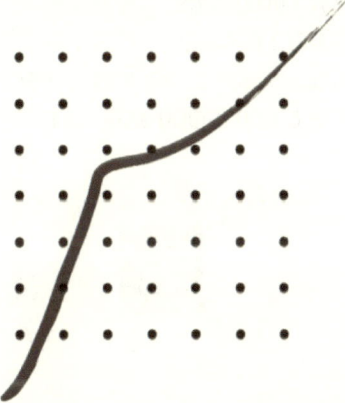

Order and deviation can be very visually striking and helps train self control. Buildings need a certain amount of regularity to remain affordable and, frankly, navigable. Deviation from the orthogonal grid holds more power when it is constrained to moments in an ordered composition.

To remind us that everything can be flipped on its head, there is also the contrast of contrast: Gradient is the opposite of contrast. It does not rely on a moment of tension to achieve its effect. It is the smooth, suggestive transition that opposes the sudden, defined transition of contrasting elements. Some spaces do not need to be divided harshly. A programmatic element may want to contrast and divide itself from certain elements and smoothly transition into other conditions. A client may want the master bedroom to be divided from the rest of the house (contrast) and open and extend out into nature (gradient). Such conditions would work with a variety of different programs and is up to the digression of the clients and the designers.

The main issues with a gradient are that it is not a strong statement and that the programs joined through this process have no clear boundary. A gradient composition will not pop visually if the entirety of the composition consists of smooth transitions. A statement must be made; otherwise, the composition cannot become striking. We also have to be careful programmatically because it can become confusing when a gradient joins two programs. The occupant can never be sure where one program ends and where another begins. As long as these conditions are taken into consideration, a gradient can be used in a composition without hindering the composition as a whole.

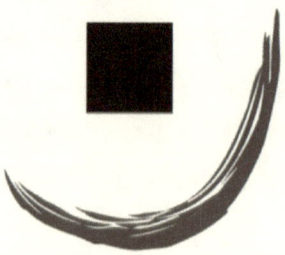

The contrast of dynamic (moving, energetic) forms and static (stationary, settled) forms can start to define the difference between transitional forms and forms defining place.

Layering

Layering is used to turn a sterile box into a habitable environment. In two-dimensional compositions, layering adds the impression of depth to a composition. It suggests multiple levels of spaces from foreground to background unifying or contrasting each other to benefit the entire composition. In levels of spaces from foreground to background unifying or contrasting each other to benefit the entire composition. In three-dimensional compositions, however, layering actually provides functional variety. A typical room consists of four walls, a floor, and a ceiling. If we regard each surface as just a two-dimensional plane with no layering, the room only allows a limited number of interactions. We can stand on the floor, sit on the floor, sit against the wall, or lean against the wall. The room can still create a spatial condition based on how the surfaces join. However, the types of engagement are limited until the room is filled with furniture, which is often compensating for the shortcomings of the architect. Furniture has its own function; it allows for plasticity of program. Layering allows an empty room to create different types of human interactions before this plasticity even occurs.

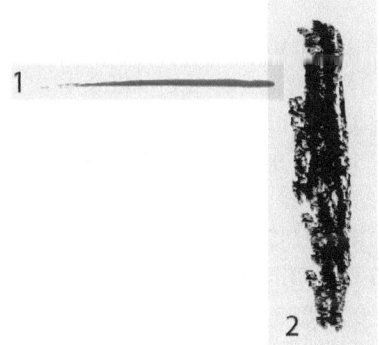

This is an example of viewing walls of a composition just as lines.

We start to think about layering by viewing each wall as a volume with thickness instead of a two-dimensional surface perceived as lines. This allows us to carve out or subdivide a wall to create layering based on functions. We need to think about every use for a wall in the program we are defining. There are hangers, shading devices, cabinets, and windows that frame views, allow privacy, create shelter, and provide other functions that change depending on program. We can even carve out from a wall to create seats for people. Windowsills can also be used for this function. Some of these functions can be achieved in one plane, but many require different layers to function properly. A shading device functions better with more separation from the rest of the wall. A hanger for clothes will protrude and command an area of space that extends past the surface of the wall. This exercise of questioning function benefits the design by being considerate to the occupant. Occupants have various intentions to which the wall must attend.

These considerations of function that create the layering of the walls should also be used for the floor and ceiling. We should question the role of the ceiling and floor as we move between parts of our program. A uniform condition in a composition as it moves between parts of program is evidence of neglect for this question of utilization.

The main problem of layering is the act of articulating program, often placing a timeline on a building. Programs change with society; so a building signs a death certificate when it is filled with rooms tailored to only one use. The trick is to add layers of function that add to the program but work after the program changes. This gives the buildings longevity and avoids the graveyard of preserved architectural landmarks that no longer serve a purpose in the everyday life of our current society.

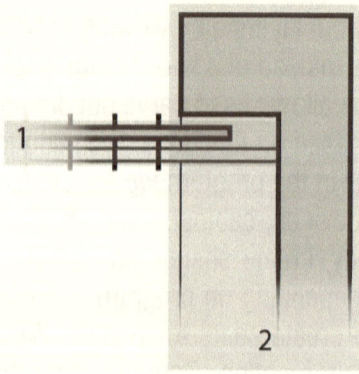

When we scale up we can utilize the thickness of each line. These walls now have multiple layers of interaction.

Alignment

Alignment creates connections. It is one of the basic methods of creating a system of organization. This hierarchy allows us to create axial and implied forms that connect program elements and bind spaces together. Order is important because our eyes find it easy to understand its logic. Our ability to understand space is directly linked to how our eyes abstract the world around us into lines so that we can understand boundary and distance. Architecture, unlike the natural world, is space that is already expressed through lines so our eyes can read the defined boundary much easier than an orchard of trees, for example. Architecture without line or alignment is without defined gestures unless the occupant is able to abstract line through visual contrast. We use alignment and line to save people from having to guess our exact intentions. This is how alignment becomes the basis for transferring our organizational intentions onto the occupant. Our eyes interpret an aligned organization of objects into a line that can become a physical and/or visual path. Axes give directionality forward and backward (an axis cannot suggest movement in only one direction because a person can either choose to walk forward along it or backward). This directionality can be used to imply a con-

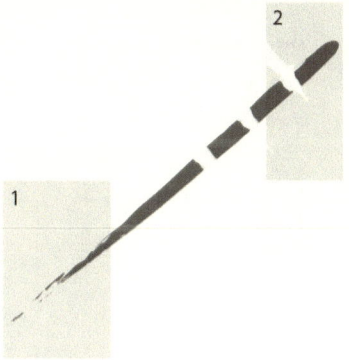

Alignment can be used to connect spaces. In this case, the alignment of the black marks creates a transitional element between the two spaces defined by the red and blue rectangles.

nection between spaces of program; so alignment is important in suggesting or controlling how to move through a space.

Another method of utilizing alignment is to bind spaces. Space is bound when walls align to create gestalt forms. As space binding increases, the definition of the form increases. This containment is particularly strong if the walls meet to define the corners. Continuity is needed or the space is unbound and will slide through the form. These two different conditions, bound and unbound space, are important when creating composition. Transitional spaces will lean towards unbound space because people need to travel through this space and into another. Places of program that want to suggest a more static environment will lean towards bound space and have more

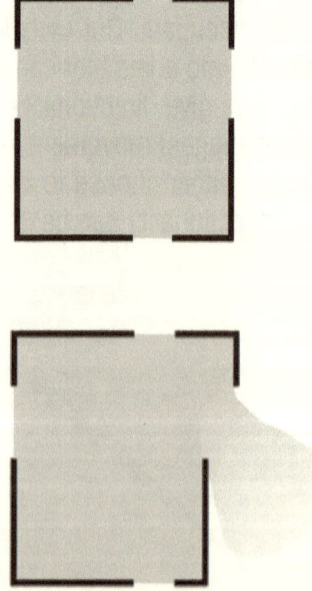

Top | *The bounding box (outer edges of the form) perfectly aligns to imply a separation between the outside and inside spaces.*

Bottom | *When alignment of the bounding box of the form is broken, the outside and inside spaces begin to mix.*

general alignment in their form. Even these spaces need a point of transition to and from the space; this is where a lack of alignment can create an excellent point of transition. Using these conditions together in a composition allows us to control the flow and setting of space in a composition.

Proportion

Proportion is another basic method of creating a sense of order in a composition. Proportion creates a visual relationship between pieces of a composition when we see a consistent variation of size between them. The stone on the floor is a fourth of the width of the hall, which is a fourth the height of the hall. A composition feels further unified when any such ratio is used. Clear areas of proportion visually seem like they belong together. Sometimes we want the whole composition to read as one. Other times we want the composition to read as several separate systems that clash together. Utilizing different proportional systems furthers the individual identity of each element in such a composition. Proportion does not have to be exact. People will not notice when we have a 10' by 10' space next to a 20' by 19'8" space. It just has to be close enough to for a general ratio of sizes to be evident.

We can also derive compositional depth depending on where we derive our proportion. There are two main arguments for proportional logic that hold some weight (in my opinion). The first is having a proportion based on the dimensional properties of the materials we buy. This can reduce the amount of wasted material and time in a project because it can eliminate the need to cut down materials from their standard lengths. The second is having a proportional system based on the human body. This method can create relationships between the person and the structure. This creates a sense of scale that will be discussed in the next few paragraphs. This method has some underlying issues but is generally used in an effort to make architecture more sensitive to the human condition.

Either of these systems will better benefit the composition than designing with a random proportion. Do not get tricked by things like the golden ratio. Serving no additional practical or experiential purposes, the golden ratio does not provide a proportional logic that is any better then a random selection of numbers to create proportion. The main two systems mentioned should be easy, quick solutions for designing proportionally. (If you can think of any other principles or elements that provide added function or value when used as a proportional system, please let me know!)

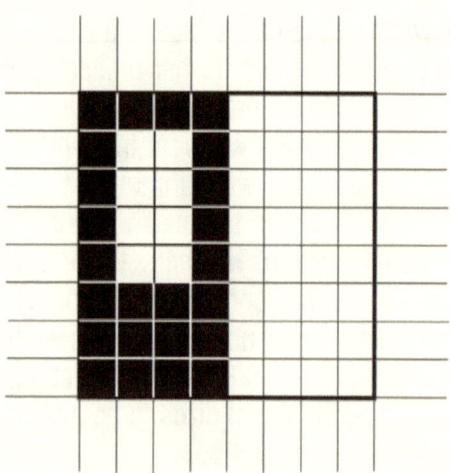

When we scale up we can utilize the thickness of each line. These walls now have multiple layers of interaction.

Scale

Scale is important in regards to the experience of architecture. We could not imagine ourselves inside a space without a sense of scale. Scale is similar to proportion because it visually implies a sized relationship between two objects. In this case of scale, one of the objects is a person. We know our own height and use it as a measuring stick to compare a volume of a space to ourselves. Constantly, our minds make these comparisons: "This space is roughly twice my height,"

"This butcher's knife is too big to use as a utensil at the dinner table," and the all too common "I swear I can fit through this." All these cases involve scale. We use this in architecture to help articulate program function. A hallway's walls can be nearly touching a person's shoulders to ensure a quick transition instead of loitering, or they could be nearly ten people wide and allow for wondering and rest without interrupting traffic. Shelves and counters should be scaled so we can reach them. There is little functionality for daily use of a shelf if you have to buy a step stool just to reach it. The scale of private spaces compared to public can also come into place. Private spaces are not meant to house many people and can acquire a much more personal, individual scale, while a public space is sized depending on exactly how many people you wish to stuff into one space. There is also the monumental scale. The monumental scale can inspire awe, but it also impersonalizes a space. Only the truest epitomes of hubris can feel that they command a room with ceilings that vanish from sight and walls that extend out into the distance. The rest of

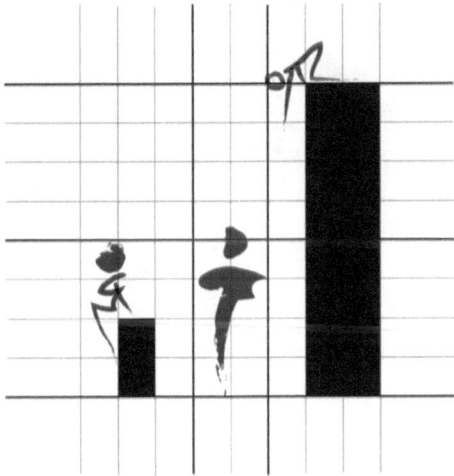

Proportion derived from an average human is a method of creating a connection between the occupant and the space. People deviate in size but proportions do not have to be perfect. It just has to be close enough.

us need to divide such a space into a more comfortable scale.

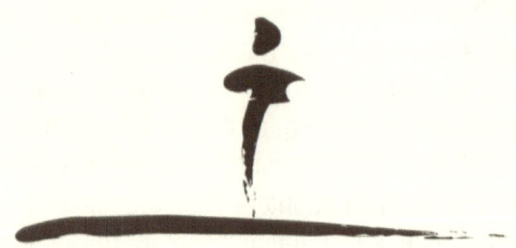

A space without consideration of human scale is limited in its depth of occupation.

A lack of comprehending scale is part of what caused Modernism to fail. When buildings combine into a superstructure and lift to open the landscape, it creates a ground plane that lacks human scale. A courtyard that is too vast and open will only be used at its edges. When we create outdoor spaces, we must remember to subdivide to create spaces for small groups of people. Some spaces should be scaled for one or two people, others up to ten, and even larger areas for games and activities that require larger groups. If a wide variety of scales are reached, then the space is more likely to be successful. This rule works because people are all extremely different in personality. More people slip through the cracks and into neglect when we cater to one personality type. The lack of scale variety, for which I often blame Modernism, has been the killer of social space.

This brings us to the issue of using human figures as a proportion system. There is no one set of numbers that come together to make the human body. We all come in different sizes, just like we all enjoy different types of social interactions. At best, we can take the average height and build of a population into consideration. This means that every proportion will be relative and we have to have some give in the proportion to accommodate extreme cases. This difference shouldn't be too noticeable because most people are not accurate at eyeballing the difference between a six-foot and a five-foot and six inches wall. The only noticeable difference should be when alternating between adult and child scales. Some programs have spaces that are designated for children and require a smaller scale than adults. With children, there can be more play with scale in order to exercise their imaginations. Most things will end up smaller so the children feel like the space belongs to them. Yet, increasing the scale of other objects, like making a two-foot tall apple, can fill children with wonder and offer more opportunities for play. These factors all tie into the challenge of designing for the human body and hopefully provoke some play with scale.

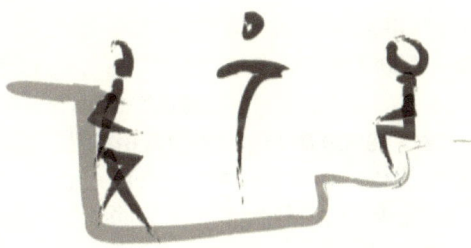

A space aware of the human scale is broken up to consider different forms of occupation. The room allotted to standing, sitting, leaning, or even laying down should be carefully considered and depend on the type of program.

Grid

Grid is the final term for creating system on the list. Grids are useful for creating rhythm in a composition and allowing us to incorporate a structural logic. Rhythm works with scale in a composition to give us a unit of measurement. Imagine that we are standing in a hallway with columns running even down either side of the hall. We subconsciously compare the distance between the first two closest columns and use that to judge the distance of a hallway. Without the columns, the empty hallway would have no sense of scale, and we would have difficulty guessing how long it is. This rhythm also gives a very basic repetitive order to our system. We can think of our structure like a piece of music. The beat of the drum is the rhythm that orders the rest of the piece. Every once in a while, a solo is thrown in to mix things up and create a more dynamic sound. This method creates ordered systems that are occasionally broken to create contrast. This actually translates into a sound structural logic. For economic reasons, it does not make much sense to have a large amount of structural variation. However, giving the majority of a structure a repetitive grid, and then only deviating during special moments, is an affor able way of having spatial diversity without being unrealistic with costs. The opposite condition is variation with moments of order. When money is not an issue, we can try such options; but it is more difficult to make this reversal look like a system. The amount of clashing elements makes the project noisy. Such partis can be counterproductive when a main goal is having a clear system of organization that allows us to navigate a building. Grids are the starting point of this organization and fill this niche well as far as combining practicality when both concept and structure are concerned. |

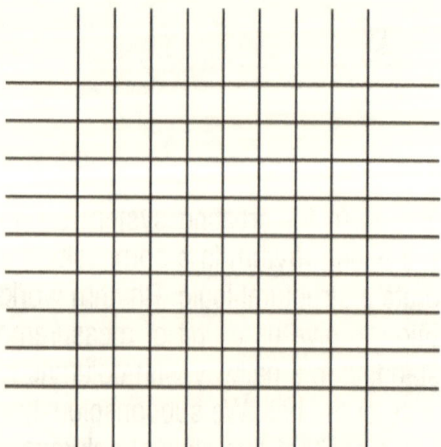

Grid is the easiest of the concepts to utilize. Imposing a grid on the site helps to create a structural logic, rhythm, and alignments.

"Between the sphere and the box, there are a number of forms that build up to completely define space. This concept can be used to help articulate our design ideas more acutely."

PERCEIVING FORM

Abstraction is the key to unlocking how we perceive form.

Without our ability to abstract the world, we could not define and separate it into different spaces.

Our brain takes a world filled with tone and contrast and turns it into edges that define depth and boundary. Edges lead to the creation of lines. Trees on the side of a field can define edge through contrast; but marking a line in the dirt or constructing a linear wall manifests this understanding of edge into a defined moment where two conditions are separated. Before we place this line at the edge of the field, it is up to the individual to speculate on the placement of an edge that separates the two spatial conditions. No two people will draw the same line to separate the forest and the field. Some will say the edge occurs where the canopy of the tree casts a shadow on the ground; others will say it starts at the tree trunk, and the edge begins as soon as the trees come into sight. Different spatial conditions are created depending on where the edge is placed--whether it is on the side of this particular field or in a building. As architects, it is our job to decide where to place these edges to design our compositions.

Breaking up shapes, used in a design parti, into lines is an

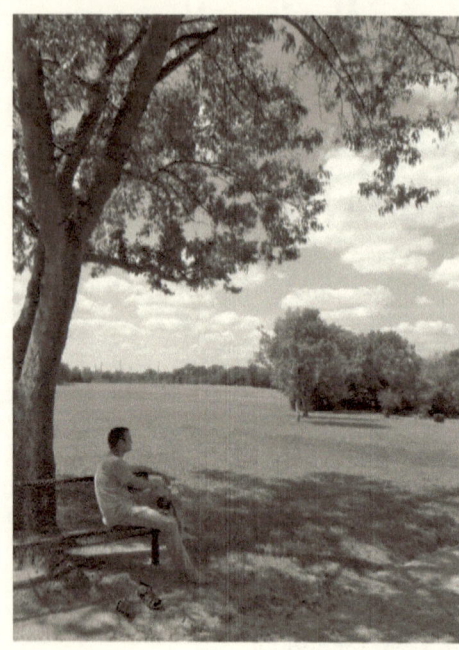
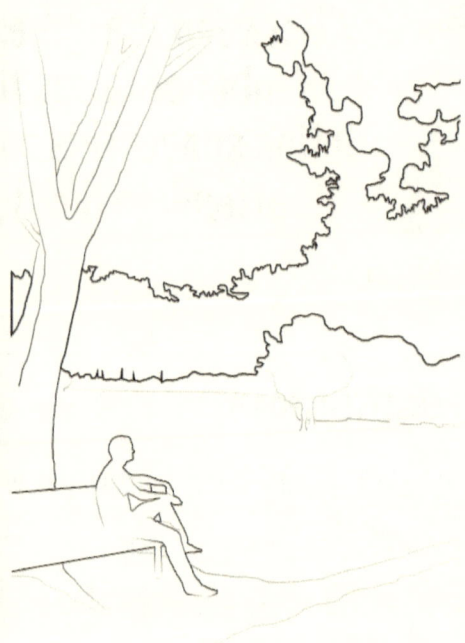

Above, Left | The world before abstraction into line is just color and tone. It is up to the individual to interpret boundaries. Feel free to take the image and turn it into a line drawing. Then see the similarities and differences between how you and I create a hierarchy of edges.

Above, Right | The previous image abstracted into line. This is only my version of the scene. Everyone will abstract the original image differently. However, now that it is abstract, I can communicate how I want the space to read.

important spatial exercise. For example, the commonly used rectangle has four faces and should be seen as a combination of four separate lines. The external and internal conditions affecting space represented by the rectangle are different for each face; therefore, each face should be expressed differently. Each line representing a wall will change depending on which direction the edge of the shape is facing. Abstracting buildings into lines adds more detail to the composition than simply drawing them as shapes.

The shape of a box broken down into lines responds to external or internal conditions.

Enclosure of space is the beginning of separating space, or at least it is the physical separation. Enclosure and defined space--space that has visual limits--are actually two completely different concepts. This realization came from "Into the Heart of Lightness" by Randy Kennedy of the New York Times. We should not limit ourselves to only architectural media. Doug Wheeler, the spatial artist in the article, made a rounded room, painted it white, and filled it with light. Participants would hesitate before entering because they perceived it as a flat wall instead of an entrance to a room. This phenomenon shows us how important edges are to defining space. Without edges, we cannot define the depth of a space; it becomes a space without limits of separation.

So to create a perfect enclosure without definition, we need a form with or without the implication of edge. That form would be a sphere. From the inside, a sphere has no gesture because its surface is evenly spaced from its center point. No matter what the lighting is, a person cannot perceive direction or depth inside this spherical space. From the outside, the sphere marks a point but still does not give directional gestures. This

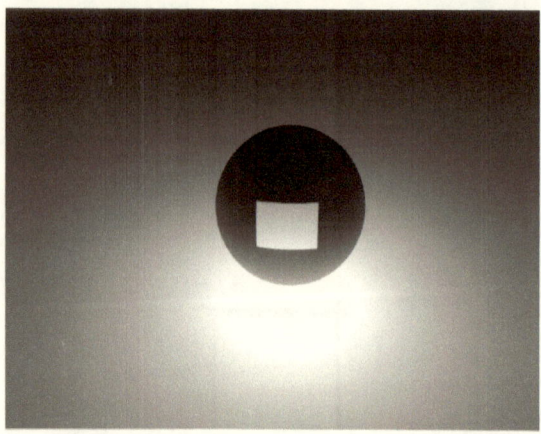

The shape of a box broken down into lines responds to external or internal conditions.

is because the contrast of the form with its surroundings implies an edge. But that edge remains constant the entire way around the form. There is no way to find the original place from which we started by just using a point on a sphere for guidance. The spatial qualities of the sphere give us a starting place to study other curved forms.

Between the sphere and the box, there are a number of forms that build up to completely define space. This concept can be used to help articulate our design ideas more acutely. The first curved form with any definition is the teardrop. The teardrop defines one point in space, while a line is formed from what we will call the "axe head," and the dome creates the first flat plane. This plane is particularly powerful because it establishes a datum that divides the realm of occupation beneath from the ceiling above. Above the datum, the edgeless form of the dome implies boundless space beyond. Curves are great to use in contrast with heavy materials for this reason. When underground or when using stone, curves add a weightlessness and openness because of their lack of definition. The next step is to cut another plane through the form. A corner is created where the two planes collide, giving directionality to the space contained in the form. From the inside, the space will appear contained in that corner and open up towards the curved space. The curved side will appear more comfortable for people who prefer larger spaces because it will appear more open. The addition of planes will continue to add definition to the space until it is completely contained. There are, however, many more variations that take place between forms with definition, like the teardrop, and forms without any definition, like the sphere.

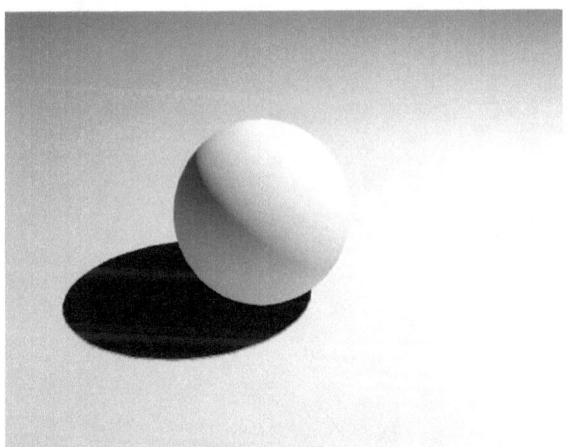

Above | *Sphere: form without direction gesture*

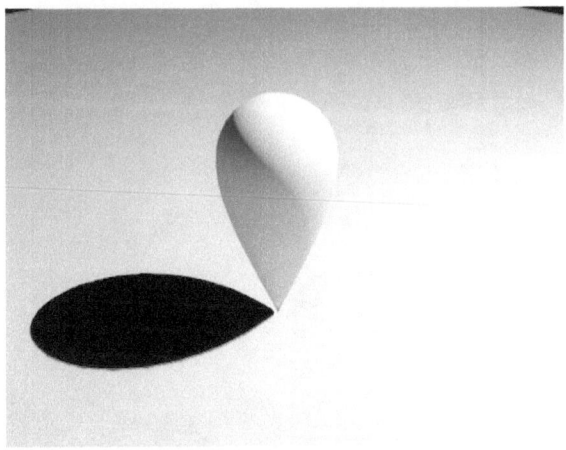

Above | *Teardrop: form defining only one point*

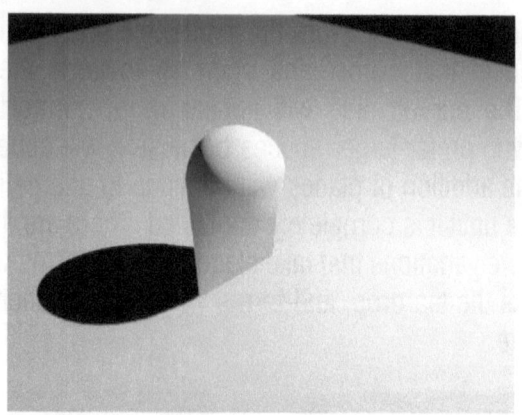

Above | *Axe head: form defining only one line*

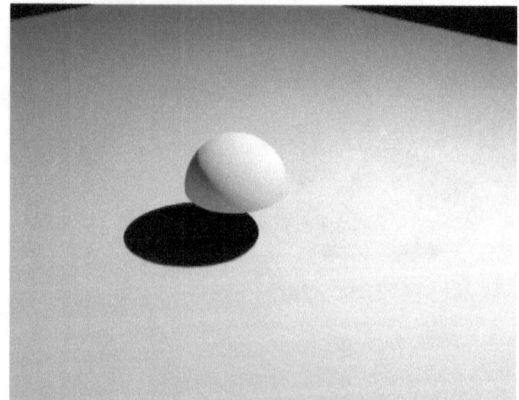

Above | *Dome: form defining only one plane*

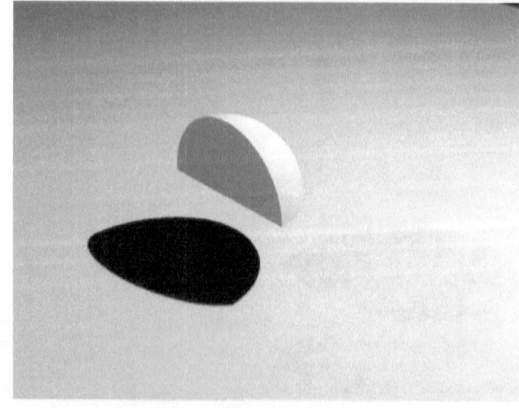

Above | *Half-Dome: form defining two planes*

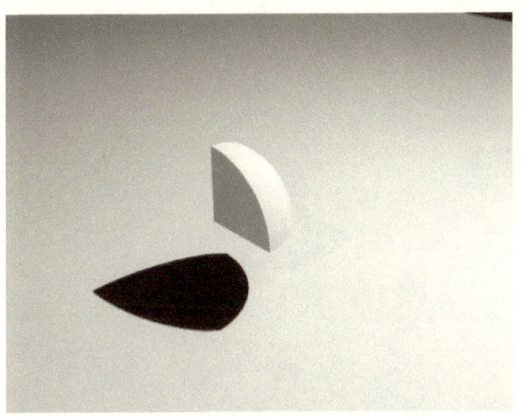

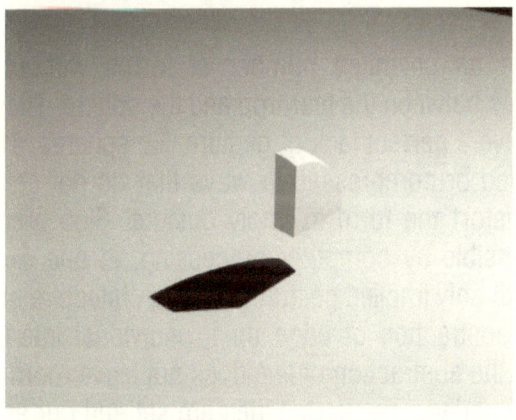

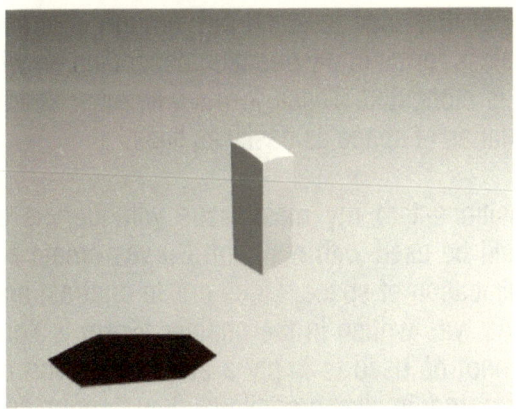

The addition of planes continues until it forms a box with all sides are perfectly defined.

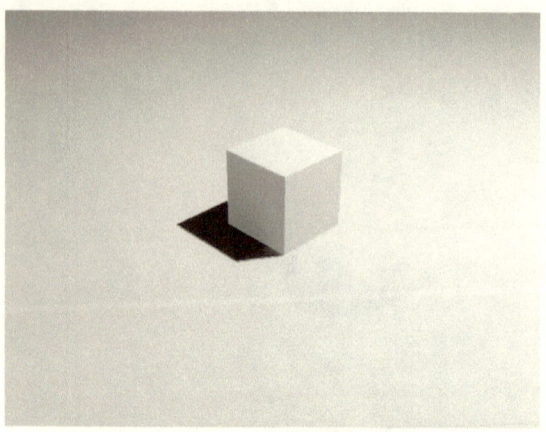
Box: all boundaries are perfectly defined by straight lines.

There are an unlimited number of forms without defined boundaries between the teardrop and the sphere. These forms do not have a perfect lack of gesture like spheres. They have been pulled or compressed in ways that do not create edge but do distort the form to imply gesture. Blob architecture, made possible by computer processing, is one example of space with only implied gestures. Blob architecture still leaves the true abstraction of edge up to individual interpretation. Spatially, the abstraction of line does not leave room for interpreting boundary. The boundaries are set and our awareness of them depends on the proximity of the edge to our eye and the ability of that edge to stand out through contrast. Therefore, edgeless forms imply direction depending on which way the form is elongated. These forms will never strictly define the boundaries of space as easily as lines.

This transitions into my main issue with curves and why they should be used with restraint. Curves create a gradient and simplification of space. Lines create contrast and abrupt change. As was written in the chapter "Form is Form," gradients cannot be used to imply a strict separation of space. Curving a corner implies a continual flow through space. The edge of a corner conveys a clear transition into a new condi-

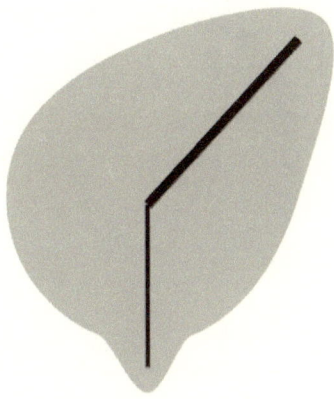

This blob implies two directions of movement. These were abstracted into the lines to show which one is the stronger gesture. A diagram of lines placed in a sphere is an excellent way to start molding an edgeless form.

tion. So, like any other gradient, curves cannot be used to define strict separation between spaces. It is also a simplification of space. Unlike a square, a circle only has one edge. Instead of being able to transform to the four different spatial conditions surrounding a square, the circle can only be tailored to one condition. This does not mean that curves cannot be used. Curves can work just fine in a composition, but they need to be used with straight lines.

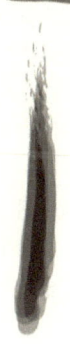

An edge is where two planes meet. The meeting of these two planes becomes a composition in and of itself. How do two planar conditions meet? This question is always essential in creating defined space.

The curve is not as complex as a corner. Instead of two conditions starkly meeting, the curve is either one condition's flawless continuation or a smooth gradient between two conditions.

The geometrical thought behind the integration of curves into an orthogonal composition is relatively simple. Curved forms combine well with orthogonal lines in two main ways. Any curve will accept a line that is tangent to it. This should be true whether it is a wavy line or a circle. Circles and similar forms can also be aligned on axis from their center point. As long as this line passes through the center of the circle, there is minimal formal tension. Formal tension is when geometries create sharp angles when they meet. Any other line passing through the circular form has increasing formal tension the farther away it is from the center point.

This exploration could create more questions than answers. It is meant as a starting point to lead us to ponder the use of forms that we are now capable of making. Form has come full circle. The perfection of handcrafted labor gave us an endless variety of forms that were lost during mass production. Now mass customization is starting to give us formal play again. What are new methods for producing form? What are methods of creating edgeless forms? Where do forms completely devoid of edge belong? What are the programs that desire edgeless form? How do we integrate them into a linear system? What is the right scale to apply to them? At what point does a curve become sharp enough read as edge? |

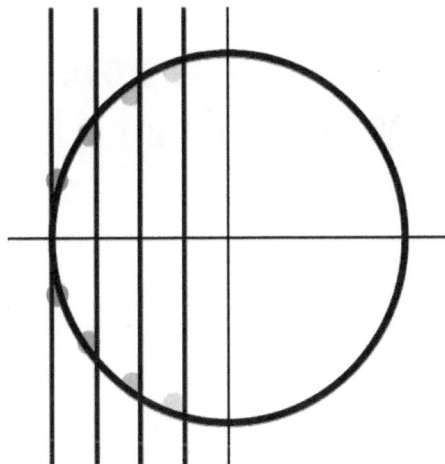

Above | *Passing through the center, orthogonal lines have the least amount of formal tension with curves. The red expresses formal tension. The most formal tension occurs when the orthogonal lines are tangent to the circle.*

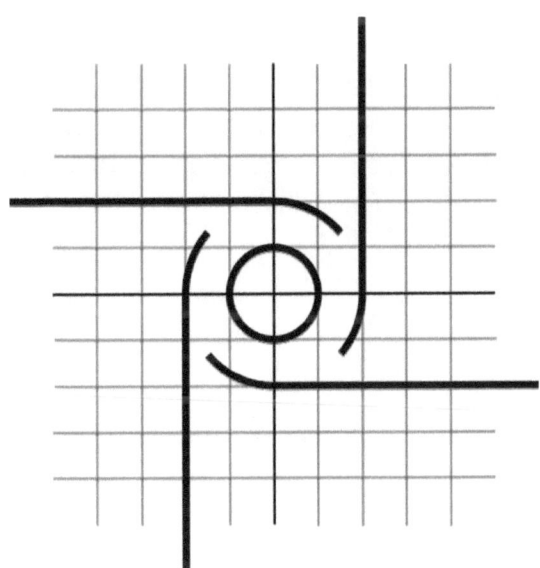

Above | *The lines are tangent to the original circle. We can use the formal tension between the curve and the orthogonal lines to create compression and release by breaking the circle into four curves.*

"We can always start by going back over our old drawings to see how we can improve our old work; then try playing with it during future designs."

FORMAL TENSION

In the first article, I discuss strategies for creating systems. However, I did not go in depth about the conflict between two different orders. Lines running perpendicular to each other are considered to be of the same system because of the symmetry of the angles created from the two lines and the lack of acute, dynamic angles. They make up the grain and cross-grain of one system. While they serve different functions inside the system, they are seen as working together through their balance. Lines that are not orthogonal to each other create new systems. There is one true exception to this: a non-orthogonal shape used as a module. It creates a singular system through repetition; however, non-orthogonal lines in this system still

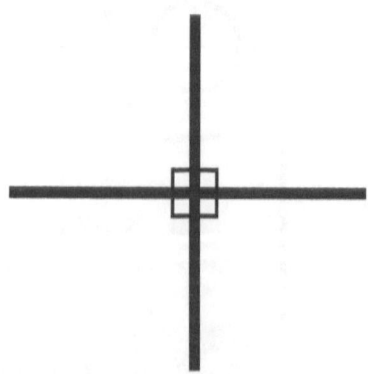

This diagram shows the balance of orthogonal lines.

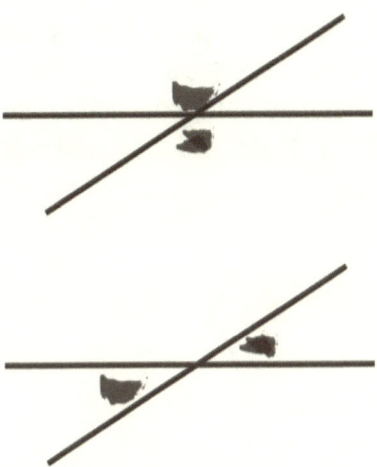

The intersection of these non-orthogonal lines has both obtuse, gentle angles highlighted in blue (top) and acute, sharp angles in red (bottom).

follow all of the geometric rules of other non-orthogonal lines.

The greatest concern for more complex geometries is the misuse of formal tension. Formal tension is created when geometries meet at sharp angles. The misuse of sharp angles can lead to the creation of dead spaces and messy compositions whose lack of order is confusing and stressful. Orthogonal lines represent the perfect balance between acute angles with high formal tension and obtuse lines with low formal tension because they create right an gles. The degree of formal tension also influences the edges that a form conveys. The contrast of obtuse angles is low and the resulting corner reads less like a threshold and more like a smooth transitional moment. Acute angles create high visual contrast between the two walls and are thus more defined. This makes areas shaped by acute angles the visual focus of a composition. The conflict is more apparent. To use these conditions properly, we have to take into account what part of the composition wants to be a unified system and which areas want to stand apart as either gentle deviations or stark contrasts.

High formal tension holds a place in thresholds, transitions, and places that require high levels of restlessness and aggression (wherever that may be). Acute angles are easier to see than right or obtuse angles; so they work better when in a stark threshold.

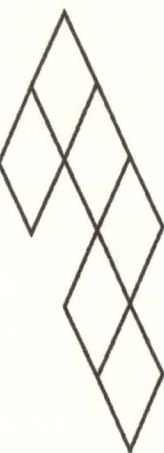

Here we have a non-orthogonal shape that still reads has being part of one system through repetition and the lack of differentiation between the lines that form the shape.

Thresholds are boundaries between two separate spaces and acute angles are the meeting of two strongly opposing systems. When the difference between these two conditions is formally expressed, the exact edge that defines the threshold is more apparent because edge protrudes closer towards the occupant. Depending on the type of transition that we want to create, there are varying degrees of restlessness we want within our transition.

Transitions with low formal tension are easier to occupy, so they do not have the same restlessness of areas with high formal tension. Though it should be noted that there are other ways to create restlessness in a transition: improper scale, lighting, and over-exposure to elements.

Places tend to want low formal tension because the idea of

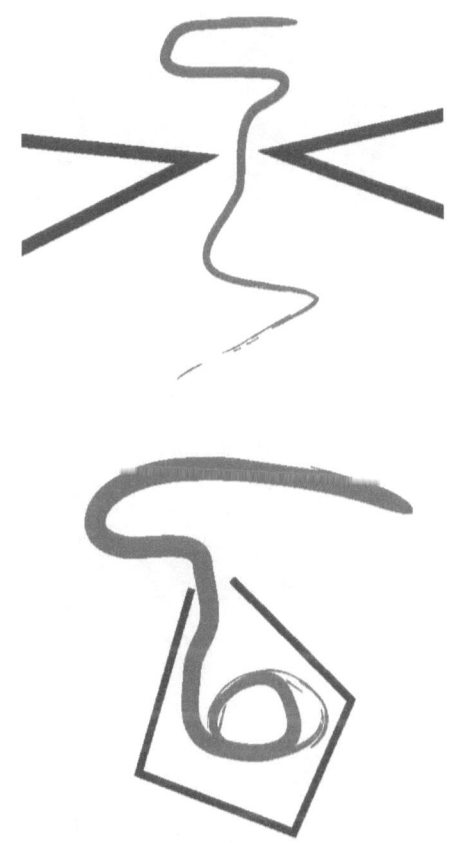

Top | *The compression and moment of threshold is created from two acute angles coming together.*

Bottom | *A space opens up on the acute angle to avoid the appearance of what we often call "dead cat spaces."*

place tends to deal with extended occupation of a space. When a place has an acute angle it either turns into the threshold for a transitional space or it has to be articulated with program by the architect. With mass production, affordable furniture is primarily orthogonal. Everyday furniture is unable to fit into tight corners; so every tight corner that is not functioning as a transitional space can be viewed as extra cost for the client and time devoted by the architect to define the space. It creates a higher level of formal determinism.

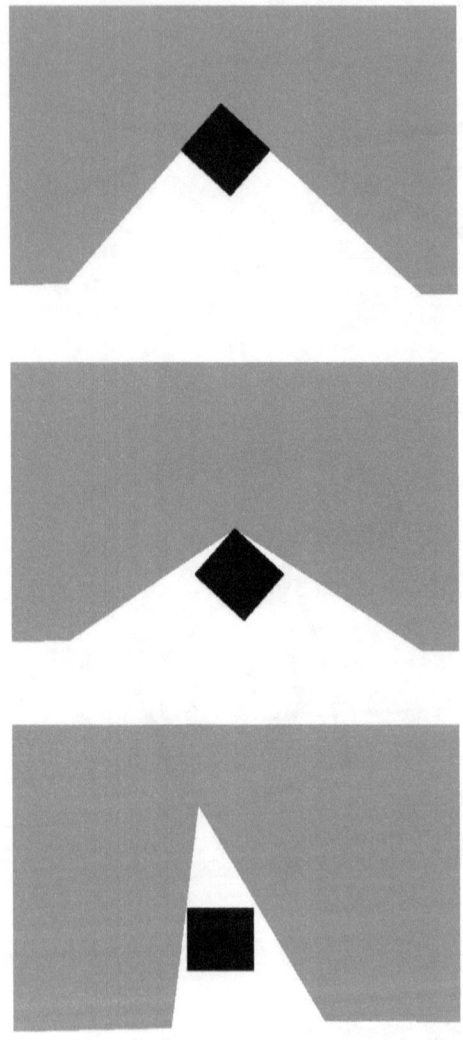

Top | *In orthogonal compositions, normal inexpensive furniture will fit properly into a corner without wasted space.*

Middle | *In obtuse corners, furniture has extra space however this can still lead to unused space between the furniture and the wall and requires special consideration. However it is still less of a problem then the acute angle.*

Bottom | *In acute corners, we see the creation of dead space that cannot fit normal furniture and needs special consideration.*

Formal determinism is the degree to which architecture defines the occupation of a space. Works by Mies van der Rohe represent a low degree of formal determinism while works by Frank Lloyd Wright represent a high degree of formal determinism. We should seek a happy middle ground between these extremes.

Systems are used for a reason and breaking the logic of these systems should always be justified and fully vetted for a successful composition. A more complex system, than that with which we create orthogonal order, is a sound place to start for geometric deviation. Site context should be the driver of external influence. The existing site lines, environmental conditions, current paths and axes, as well as adjacent buildings are rather justifiable reasons for making non-orthogonal lines in a composition. While they may not enforce a unity to the project, embrace the dynamic nature of these conditions and use it to your advantage. When we look outwards and address the site, we can backtrack and create internal complex geometries that are only justified by the desired conditions of our compositions. Corbusier is known for using these internally justified strategies. An inspection of la Tourette's plan shows us a regulated scheme with planned moments of deviation that work within his composition. A moment of deviation inside a strict order is just one element within a parti. On the opposite end of the spectrum, architects purposefully create a mess with moments of order. Any variation that falls between, or outside of, these polar conditions should be even more justified than breaks in the system made to accommodate the site conditions. Site conditions have to be addressed for a building to function; but experiential considerations can be viewed as added benefit each time one is made. Each non-orthogonal line, in such cases, needs more than one justification for its existence. When speaking of our designs, we should be able to say, "This deviation has to be here because of A, B, and C." |

JULIE EIZENBERG

Each semester begins following a familiar format: an accomplished architect stands before us to inspire and motivate our malleable minds. These speakers herald grand concepts, exquisitely cast material palettes and even prophecies of our industry's future. Julie Eizenberg's presence earlier this month was refreshingly unique. She spoke of admittedly unacademic architectural considerations that demonstrated her humanist sensitivities and that reveled in the often messy struggles of realizing architecture. We are compelled to share our brief research of Julie and her firm in hopes of perpetuating a conversation around her methodologies.

Julie and her firm's founding partner, Hank Koning, continue to be deeply influenced by the unique techniques and trends of their surroundings.

"Despite the Australian roots of its founders, there is something quintessentially Southern Californian about the firm's sensibility. Or maybe it's because of those roots: Los Angeles architecture has always thrived by making a place for ambitious, eccentric, and forward-looking émigrés from all over, whether it was Rudolph Schindler and Richard Neutra from Vienna or Frank Gehry, born Frank Goldberg, from Toronto. Certainly, Koning and Eizenberg's taste for combining frugality and verve in the same project, and for juxtaposing serious

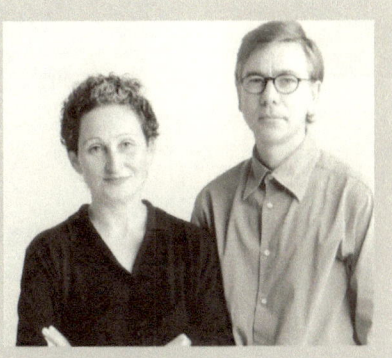

architectural ideas with informality and references to Pop Art, flows directly out of a singularly L.A. tradition. Their work— which ranges from single-family residential projects to afford- able housing to commissions from cultural, civic, and non- profit clients—wraps joy, smarts, improvisational flair, and resourcefulness together in the same colorful package. Like much of the meaningful architecture in this city, it stakes out a happily anti-perfectionist stance, finding its meaning in the gaps between abstract goals and achievable ones."

-MetropolisMag.com, "The Right Touch" by Chris Hawthorne

While clearly influenced by these trends of Los Angeles archi- tecture of the twentieth century, Koning Eizenberg is free of any dogmatic adherence to them.

"The through-line in [Koning Eizenberg's] work is that they are not bringing preconceived notions to bear. It's really about seeing what's needed at a certain point in time, the specific constraints and forces arrayed in front of them, and how they can respond."

-Mark Robbins, Dean of Syracuse Architecture School

Koning Eizenberg's Children's Museum in Pittsburgh demon- strates their approach to usage designations, or lack thereof.

"Disorder attracts Hank Koning and Julie Eizenberg...For the architects, designing for kids means engaging them, not controlling them. Instead of structures that thwart vandals and assuage insurance inspectors, buildings that encourage messy vitality are their specialty. In the museum, as well as a handful of other commissions for schools, parks, and community centers, the architects demonstrate a healthy disrespect for authority.

They believe that if buildings are to succeed as social spaces, they must be armatures for discovery: not dictating specific responses but providing opportunities for the widest range of experiences."

-MetropolisMag.com, "Project Play" by Andrew Blum

"These artful, upbeat buildings belie the social and economic forces often stacked against them. Yet KEA's relentless reinventions—of materials, forms, assemblies, and business partnerships—are paying off.

'Ten years ago the question was how to get housing providers to see there's value in what architects can do. That's well-proven at this point. Now the deal is how to get to the sweet spot of aligning design and budget. Some cities allow you to do it smarter than others, but it's still tough to get the right values integrated with code.'

'Whether it's cross-breezes, colorful window graphics, or the inclusion of hands-on gardens that foster social trust, KEA's buildings have the power to change everyday lives. The prospect clearly energizes Eizenberg. "Multifamily and mixed-use housing represents a stimulating set of ideas," she says. "The people running these organizations all believe architecture is the key to social change. There is a lot afoot."'

-Residential Architect, "Koning Eizenberg Architecture" by
Cheryl Weber, LEED AP

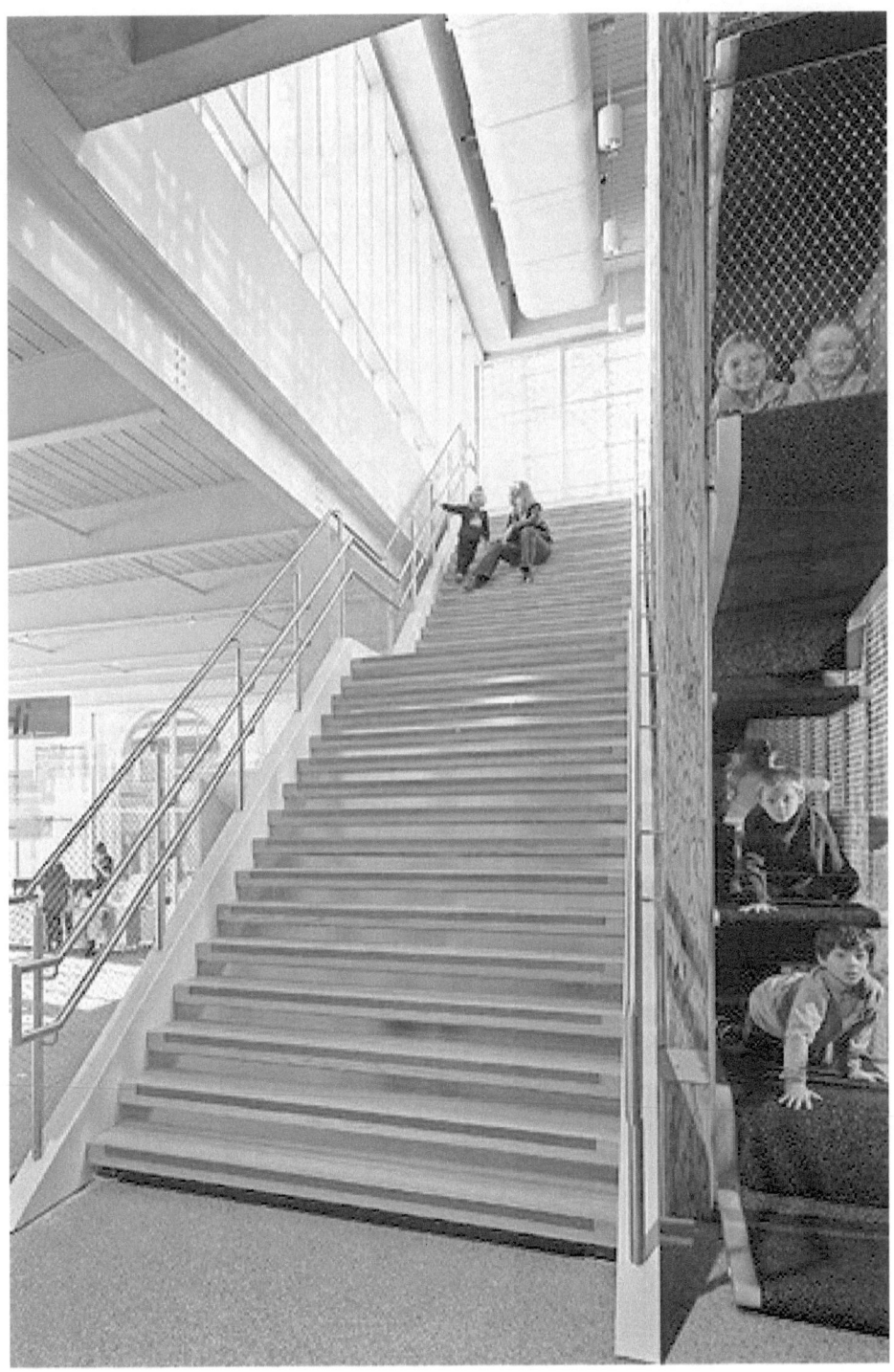

Above | *Children are at play in the interior of Koning Eizenberg's Children's Museum in Pittsburgh*

> "...I was delighted to see Julie, as an architect, discuss public space; something I fear is lost in many architecturally-centered conversations"

ANALYSIS BY KEIHLY MOORE

Since starting the urban design program, I've paid much more attention to public space. In fact, these days, public space is always on my mind. In Julie Eizenberg's lecture on the first day of class, I was delighted to see Julie, as an architect, discuss public space; something I fear is lost in many architecturally-centered conversations. I'll highlight a few of the thoughts that stuck with me from her lecture with the hopes that will hopefully influence future design work. Ultimately, one of our roles as designers is to be place makers.

She spoke about public space as experience, more than a collection of activities. She advocated for various interaction layers and intersections, while still keeping an atmosphere of informality. How can we design the opportunity for things to happen?

Prescriptive places, places that are designed purposely for a specific use or clientele, are not designed to flex.

Flexibility is one of the most important characteristics of a successful public space.

Recall the last time you walked through an active public space and something was happening there that hadn't been there before, whether it was a festival, a market, or new people to watch. Next time you walk through, notice the designed informality that allows these various activities to occur.

Another notable concept was that of the East Asian idea of borrowed landscapes. In a project in Seattle, Eizenberg "borrowed" the distant mountain landscape for construction in her competition idea. She used design elements to frame the distant view, allowing the surroundings to ground the immediate place.

This is a reminder to be cognizant of the place you're in, thinking beyond lot lines.

Always be aware of what's around you.

While I write about Julie, I am also filtering concepts that have become part of my thesis work. One of the most important rules is to layer, encourage overlaps, and combine functions and purposes. I'm focusing on turning green infrastructure into public infrastructure, so that the duties of each can additively perform. |

DESIGN AND CONSTRUCTION
WILL PHILEMON

Last semester, Will studied the Avant-Garde movement and how it could influence architecture. He was in a class that asked the question "Can architecture be Avant-Garde?" During his research, he was drawn to the state of today's' construction process and wondered what the Avant-Garde artists of the 1920's would do to change it. From there, he looked at different kinds of people involved in any given construction project. He wanted to find a way to better integrate all of their contributions in order to streamline the construction process.

His focus began to shift from the construction process to design in general. He became interested in discovering others' perspectives in all aspects of design. So, his topic became more about working collaboratively and how students may take advantage of each others' specialties by working together.

Will believes this topic is important because it opens up many new ways for us to work with others in the future. "We can identify many areas of design that can be improved through collaboration with others. Sometimes, a person who knows nothing about a project may provide a viewpoint that proves to be a valuable suggestion. If we can find ways to identify where these types of possibilities exist then we can fundamentally change the way we work with others to solve design problems."

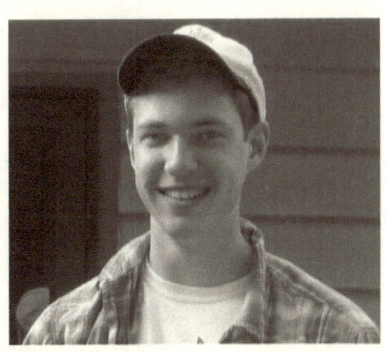

MOVING TOWARD INTEGRATION

Architecture is one of the few art forms where the production of the work is separated from its creator. The act of constructing a building was largely affected by the division of labor and has since become highly industrialized. As a result, the production and construction of architecture has become heavily reliant on other trades. In a 1924 article, Mies Van Der Rohe said that this was one of the key problems facing architects.

Contemporary construction practices have shaped the building industry into a type of assembly line where the architect designs something and then turns it over to someone else to build it. Granted, there is usually a high level of consultation between the architect and the other professionals involved, but there is also a dependency on them. Many would argue that the only way to avoid this sort of process is for the architect to return to being the master craftsman and not only design a building but construct it too. This way, the architect would have control over the entire process from start to finish. In the same article, Mies says,

> "Anyone who might regret that the house of the future will no longer be produced by craftsmen should recall that the automobile is no longer built by wheelwrights either."

Mies is saying that industrialization has affected almost everything in our lives from our houses to our cars. The expert designer does not build the things he designs; instead, the expert builder constructs things he does not design.

When Mies spoke on this subject he called for a "fundamental change in the building industry." One way to do this is to change the way that architects, engineers and contractors work with each other. How much influence should each of them have on each other's respective part of a project? Who is ultimately considered the author of a building? Perhaps the architect should consider the work of the engineer and contractor as a part of the buildings' design.

Imagine if the process of construction, the part we as students often overlook, is integrated into the parti of a project.

This idea is in effect a search for a more unified process between design and construction. I am currently gathering information from Charlotte area architects, engineers and contractors to gain a further understanding of how the three interact and communicate with each other. This information will then serve as the basis to find the best way to improve this process for the benefit of the actual building that is produced by it. |

"The expert designer does not build the things he designs; instead, the expert builder constructs things he does not design."

WORKING COLLABORATIVELY

As I search for a way to integrate architectural design and construction, I find that their inherent connection runs much deeper than I previously thought. I believe that this increases the likelihood that they can both influence one another. I have recently consulted architects, engineers, contractors and project managers who have brought several new pieces of information to my attention regarding this matter.

First, I wanted to gain a better understanding of how the various professionals who might be a part of any given project work together. The main thing here, which was a bit of a formality, dealt with communication. Everyone I spoke to made it clear that accessibility and attitude are the most important factors when it comes to working with someone in another field. Now, this isn't particularly exciting for us a designers, and future architects, but it was stressed so much that I couldn't leave it out.

Now, time to get into the more interesting part. When I mentioned my idea about integrating design and construction, I received a common response from almost everyone I spoke with. I was told that it is possible, but that it is a skill that must be learned. They said that working with others, and working with others effectively, must be practiced, and should be practiced before entering the professional work environment. In other words, it must be done in school. Learning how to coordinate with other students is no different than learning how to coordinate with other professions.

And when I say "other students," I mean students who aren't architecture students; students who have different backgrounds and who work in different ways.

Designing, planning, even talking, with different types of students can prove to be very difficult. This is an obstacle for us that must be removed if we want to have any chance at integrating their ideas and insights into our projects.

This in turn brings up an important set of concerns. What are the ramifications for us if we include, for example, engineering students into our studio project processes? It seems logical to assume that we would be limiting ourselves in terms of what we would be able to do design-wise. Many feel that in architecture school you should be able to exhaust the possibilities of a design, without concern of the engineering, so that you can learn a way in which to think. This is a valid thought; however, all of the architects I spoke with said that the input from other professionals was helpful to them in their design process and that it never seemed to inhibit them.

So, should we as students start seeking out our peers in other disciplines and ask them to help us with our projects?

No. Not at this point; but I do think that we are closer to finding a way to integrate all processes of design. We can't ex pect to work exclusively and have a seamless project. It is also not enough to occasionally meet and discuss a problem. Everyone who is a part of a project must work together, collectively, throughout the entirety of the project in order for our influences to mesh. Any studio project could be considered as collective and multi-disciplinary at any stage, not just the beginning, middle or end. Students of different disciplines can work hand in hand to discover new approaches to architecture at every scale rather than just solve each other's problems.

Example.

The EPA is holding a competition called P3 (People, Prosperity, and the Planet) which will take place at the National Sustainable Design Expo in Washington DC later this year. UNC Charlotte is participating by submitting a design for an algae façade system which will serve as a high performance alternative to the popular glass façade. The School of Architecture offers a class where students are working to research, design and fabricate a prototype façade for the competition.

> The class, which I am a part of, works with students from the Engineering Technology, Mechanical Engineering, Construction Management and Biology departments at UNC Charlotte.

There is also a strong working relationship with various types of professionals and professors who are providing practical insights into the project.

By working on this project, I have seen firsthand the merits of working together and the perils of trying to make that happen. It is certainly difficult to coordinate work with other students, especially when working across departments, but in doing so I have discovered how, and why, we should continue doing this. I will elaborate on the three major methods of collaboration that I have experienced during the course of the project.

- Students contact each other through email or phone and discuss what they have done and what needs to be done. This is how most of the collaboration was done in the early part of the project. I quickly found out that this method was incapable of producing good results. The work indicated that everyone was not "on the same page" during the initial conversation. This almost always results in everyone having to go back and rework what they did. That process is neither productive nor efficient.

- Students meet and begin to work on a problem before going their separate ways to finish it. This was the adopted method once the first one was found to be ineffective. Groups of students would get together and sketch/discuss problems. While this almost always cleared up the issues of what needed to be done and it resulted in the problem being solved, it didn't seem that reliable. This is because different students were doing different things, which meant that not everyone knew everything about everything.

- Students completely work through a problem together from start to finish. This is by far the most effective way to work because students are able to offer advice over multiple iterations. By working through a problem together, students are able to eliminate the need to revisit persistent problems and everyone has a good understanding of why things are done the way they are done. For example, I recently had the opportunity to work with a professional engineer from Optima Engineers in Charlotte to size the pipe and mechanical system for the algae façade. We had previously worked separately and kept running into problems; so we found a time where we could sit down and work together from start to finish. We ended up solving the problem in a matter of minutes and I feel very good about the progress we made and how we are going to move forward in the future. |

"why do contemporary architecture students (myself included) design their studio projects with standard doors and windows and make buildings that we all see built every day in the world around us?"

THE IMPORTANCE OF INTEGRATION

The more I learn about the potential benefits of interdisciplinary collaboration, the more I wonder why design students rarely reach out to other fields.

> Many possibilities are waiting in the other academic buildings spread across the campus of UNC Charlotte that could change the way we design and think forever.

Architecture students are given the unique experience of working in a studio environment that allows for the rapid exchange of thoughts and ideas. This is something that is often taken for granted and we often forget that most other students don't have this luxury. With that in mind, wouldn't it be great to use a studio inspired atmosphere to pursue a way to bring the rest of UNC Charlotte's students together for the benefit of everyone's education? Not only would this improve our university at large, it would greatly improve the value of our scholarship in the School of Architecture.

School is the perfect place to experiment with this kind of collaborative research and apply it to our studio projects. The reason why? There is no consequence for failure! In fact, the projects that cause struggles and failures are the ones most likely to create positive learning opportunities that we can carry with us into the future. Why should we not meet with students in the College of Health and Human Sciences (CHHS) to discuss the location of apertures on the ground floor of our studio project? We'll certainly never know the answer to this question if we never try. Of course, that is only one (completely random) example that I just made up, but we can push it a little farther to help illustrate my point.

For all we know, there could be some kind of revolutionary research going on in the CHHS that could be integrated into, and become a fundamental part of, our design.

The approach inspired by students in the CHHS might end up being the perfect solution for the project. It might provide us with a strategy that we will use for the rest of our careers as architects. It could also become a complete failure. The exercise could very well be an experiment that was attempted and was unsuccessful as an architectural implementation.

So what's the point? Why would we want to waste our time on an excursion that might not result in helping us make "the perfect studio project?" The reason is simple: it's not about having a perfect project. It's about learning as much as you can with your project and then moving on to the next one. Every project that we work on in school should be viewed as an exercise that is meant to help us figure out something that has given us trouble in the past. As students, there is such a vast array from which we can learn.

Our goal when we start a new project should be to identify something that we don't currently understand and use the project to research, learn, and find solutions.

That means to completely exhaust all the resources that surround us so that we can figure out a viable solution for ourselves rather than just accept the conclusions that someone else may have made about the topic. One of the most valuable resources that we have, and almost never use, is the other students at UNC Charlotte. However, the only way to take full advantage of their knowledge and expertise is to have a narrowly defined design problem that we are working on.

To conclude, I have to present one final example and ask this question: why do contemporary architecture students (myself included) design their studio projects with standard doors and windows and make buildings that we all see built every day in the world around us? We have the rest of our lives to build ordinary buildings and let standards and codes drive our designs. Recently, an architect from Charlotte told me that architecture school is not meant to teach students the technical "ins and outs" of architecture, it is meant to teach them how to think and how to design. I took that to mean that we should free ourselves of all preconceptions we have about buildings and their components so that we can actually DESIGN them!

And, in the meantime, we might as well work with as many different kinds of students that we can to help us achieve our goals.

That way, we will become better at what we do, they will become better at what they do, and we'll both become better communicators and collaborators to benefit our future careers in the professional world. |

CREDITS

"Give a man a fish and you feed him for a day. Teach a man to fish and you feed him for a lifetime."

This ancient Chinese proverb is the undertone for much of what we seek to accomplish through Gump Record. It suggests that it is more worthwhile to teach someone to do something, by sharing knowledge and skills, than do something for them.

Let's build a community where the architect teaches the homeless to build their own sufficient shelters, where the homeless teach the architect to use resources scrupulously, and where a child reignites both their imaginations and senses of wonder.

Gump Record is the vehicle that allows us to spread these perspectives and experiences across artificial boundaries. Through Gump Record, we can teach each other to fish.

Become a Contributor.
gumprecord.org

Blake Montieth | Editor/President
Tori Pike | Assistant Editor of Design
Julia Badorrek | Assistant Editor of Content
Melissa Krakowski | Vice President of Physical Distribution
Carly Coates | Vice President of Marketing/Outreach, Secretary
Gideon Gourley | Treasurer